EMOTION
ALL THAT MATTERS

EMOTION

Sandi Mann

ALL THAT MATTERS

First published in Great Britain in 2014 by John Murray Learning. An Hachette UK company.

First published in US in 2014 by The McGraw-Hill Companies, Inc.

This edition published 2014

British Library Cataloguing in Publication Data: a catalogue record for this title is available from the British Library.

Library of Congress Catalog Card Number: on file.

10 9 8 7 6 5 4 3 2 1

Paperback ISBN 978 1 47 180161 7

eBook ISBN 978 1 47 180570 7

Typeset by Cenveo® Publisher Services.

Printed and bound in Great Britain by CPI Group (UK) Ltd., Croydon, CR0 4YY.

John Murray Learning policy is to use papers that are natural, renewable and recyclable products and made from wood grown in sustainable forests. The logging and manufacturing processes are expected to conform to the environmental regulations of the country of origin.

John Murray Learning
338 Euston Road
London NW1 3BH
www.hodder.co.uk

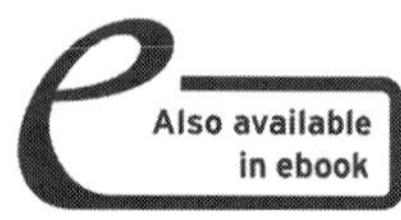

Contents

1

What are emotions anyway?

'When dealing with people, remember you are not dealing with creatures of logic, but creatures of emotion.'

Dale Carnegie

'Emotion is a potentially noble part of what it is to be human.' So says Janet Landman in an essay on emotions (Landman 1996) in which she laments that, if only Nazis such as Rudolf Höss (who commanded the Auschwitz concentration camp) had been more emotional and less rational, the atrocities of the Second World War might never have happened.

Everyone knows what emotions are – don't they? Actually, emotions are not that easy to define (try explaining the term to a small child). Are emotions things that we feel or think? Are they tied up with our behaviour or maybe our mood? Or perhaps emotions are simply chemical reactions in our bodies, as love has sometimes been described?

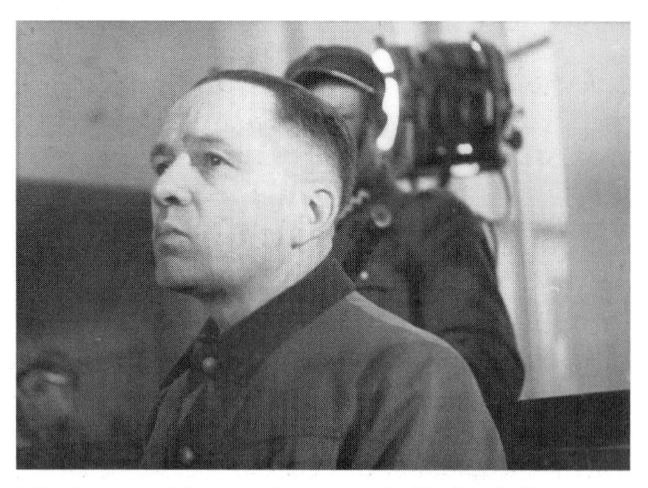

▲ **Emotions are at the root of our humanity. The Auschwitz commandant Rudolf Höss seems to have had a complete lack of emotion of any kind – feeling neither pity for his millions of victims nor fear during his own eventual execution by hanging. He even once avowed that 'the feeling of hatred is not in me'.**

The answer is that emotions are all of these things. Most researchers believe that emotions consist of five distinct components, and some believe that, to truly experience an emotion, at least four out of five components must exist (there is doubt about the fifth). These are:

1 **Our cognitions:** that is, what we think – our interpretation of events producing the emotion. For example, thinking about a sad event such as a bereavement induces sad emotions.

2 **Our feelings:** we label the way we feel as being angry, sad and so on. These feelings are very subjective and also quite personal, in that other people cannot always discern how we feel just by looking at us. The labels we give emotions are varied.

3 **Our physiological reactions:** how our bodies react (e.g. sweating, raised heartbeat, clenched fist).This includes the bodily changes that we cannot see or notice such as chemicals secreted from various glands during the experience of an emotion.

4 **Our behaviour:** such as running away, hitting someone/something, hugging someone and so on.

5 **Our expression:** this component doesn't have to be present, in that you can feel an emotion without any outward expression. However, often emotions are accompanied by a distinct change in facial and/or vocal expression (e.g. we blush when embarrassed or smile when we are happy). Such expression can also be used to deliberately convey an emotion (that is either felt or not felt) – more on this in Chapter 2.

Thus, to experience the phenomenon of an emotion that we are all so familiar with, the emotional trigger or stimulus must penetrate our consciousness; there must be some kind of reaction in our body; we produce some kind of behavioural change and we label the whole thing as an 'emotion' (and this emotion may be communicated by our outward expressions).

Incidentally, moods are different from emotions. They tend to last longer, but be of less intensity. Moods can last an entire day, or even a week, but emotions are much more transient (though felt more markedly).

Love, hate, joy... how many different emotions are there?

According to classic work by Paul Ekman (1992), there are only six distinct emotions. These are anger, disgust, fear, happiness, sadness and surprise. Another influential researcher, Robert Plutchik (2002), agreed that there were a finite number of distinct emotions but suggested that there are eight basic emotions, rather than six, and that these could be grouped into four pairs of opposites:

- joy ←——→ sadness
- trust ←——→ disgust
- anger ←——→ fear
- surprise ←——→ anticipation.

He further suggested that these primary emotions could be 'blended' (a bit like primary colours) into more complex emotions; for example, disgust and anger could blend together to form contempt. In Plutchik's view, all emotions are a combination of these basic emotions and many of the emotions that we identify are, in reality, just forms of the above eight. Thus, for example, we might claim that we are elated, thrilled, happy, delighted or even exhilarated, but all these are variations of the basic emotion of 'joy'. Similarly, rage and annoyance are forms of anger.

What is the point of emotion?

Emotions get a bad press. They are often seen as something to be regulated or managed, things that are harmful if they get out of control and something that can get us into trouble either at work or beyond. Positive emotions are seen as more acceptable than negative; anger, in particular, is seen as the bad guy of all emotions (for more on anger, see Chapter 4).

And yet, all emotions have a point to them. They played an important part in our evolutionary history and helped us survive. For example, seeing disgust on someone's face when presented with mouldy food ensured that we avoided eating something dangerous; getting bored by things that no longer presented a risk to us allowed us to divert our energy to monitoring new dangers; and being able to communicate happiness allowed beneficial social interactions to develop. Even anger was an important emotion to our ancestors, motivating us to seek food when we were hungry, to fight off predators and to compete for scarce resources.

Emotions might not have quite the same benefits in terms of our survival today (although they do help us avoid danger), but they still play an important role. They help us make friends and relax, and they motivate us to achieve, to change our lives and to right injustices in the world.

Do we act on our emotions – or do we get emotional about our actions?

It is well known that emotions are associated with a range of physical and cognitive processes, but psychologists and philosophers have been grappling with the issue of what comes first for over a hundred years. Do the physical changes in our body follow the emotion, or do we feel the emotion because of the physical changes in our body?

The psychologist William James first outlined his theory of emotion in *Mind* in 1884. Actually, he only just pipped fellow Dutch physiologist Carle Lange to the post as they both postulated the same processes as being involved. Consequently, the resulting theory is referred to as the **James–Lange theory of emotion** to acknowledge the input of both parties.

Their proposal was that emotion occurs as a direct result of physiological changes produced by the body's autonomic nervous system. You see something and this causes physical changes to occur in your body. You then interpret those changes as an emotion. For example, imagine a scary man approaches you in a dark alleyway. This external stimulus causes your heartbeat to quicken and your legs to tremble. You notice these changes in your body and decide that you must feel frightened ('I am trembling therefore I am frightened').

This theory turned on its head what was seen as the obvious sequence of events at the time. As James himself said, 'Common sense says, we lose our fortune, are sorry and weep; we meet a bear, are frightened and run; we are insulted by a rival, are angry and strike.' This, he claimed, was the incorrect order of events and, actually, we feel sorry *because* we cry, we are angry *because* we hit and we are afraid *because* we tremble. Without the physical reactions in our bodies, we might take a rational course of action to, for example, run away from the bear, but this would be an unemotional, cognitive decision, devoid of any emotion – we would not actually feel frightened unless we experienced the physical changes first.

In the 1920s Walter Cannon (who was later joined by Phillip Bard) disagreed with the James–Lange theory and put forward four main arguments to discredit it:

1 People can, in fact, experience physiological arousal *without* experiencing emotion, such as when they have been engaged in exercise. In this case, the

physiological symptoms such as increased heart rate are not indicative of emotions (e.g. fear).

2 Physiological reactions happen quite slowly, so are unlikely to be the cause of experiences of emotion since we often experience emotions quite quickly. For example, if you are alone at night in your house and hear a sudden suspicious noise, you are likely to feel afraid rather quickly, while the physical 'symptoms' of fear generally take longer to materialize.

3 People can experience very different emotions even when they have the same pattern of physiological arousal. For example, a person may have increased heart rate and feel breathless both when they are angry and when they are excited.

4 Emotion was found still to occur even when the physical changes occurring in the body could not be communicated back to the brain. Cannon conducted experiments on cats in which he disconnected the nerves giving feedback to the brain but these cats still demonstrated 'rage' when provoked (this was called 'sham rage' since, according to Lange, without feedback to the brain, they shouldn't experience real rage at all).

Together with Bard, the **Cannon–Bard theory of emotion**, as it became known, suggested that, rather than the physical reactions coming first and then producing the emotion, the two processes happen simultaneously. Some external stimulus (the sight of that scary man in the dark alleyway) will trigger the thalamus in the brain to send information simultaneously to both other areas of the brain (specifically the cerebral cortex) and the autonomic nervous system (including the skeletal muscles) so that both the awareness of emotion (in the brain) and the physical reaction (e.g. in the muscles) occur at once.

Wobbly bridges... and why we should take our date to see a scary film

More recent explanations (first put forward by Schachter and Singer 1962) accounting for the experience of emotions focus on the role played by our brain in interpreting physical sensations as emotions. It is not enough to just experience the physical reactions in our body; we must also have reason to interpret and label these changes as a particular emotion. The actual physical changes we experience may be the same for every emotion; it is our interpretation of the environment and so on that leads us to label these sensations as a particular emotion.

Imagine that you notice feeling hot and sweaty. The way you interpret these physical sensations will depend on what has happened before you noticed them:

- **Scenario 1:** Before feeling hot and sweaty, you had just sprinted 400 yards to catch a bus. You immediately assume that the physical sensations are due to your unaccustomed exercise (and you resolve to get fitter!).

- **Scenario 2:** A few minutes ago, you narrowly avoided being hit by a bus. You had been walking along, minding your own business, when the bus mounted the kerb, missing you by inches. You interpret the sweating and hot feelings as fear as you appreciate the danger you were in.

- **Scenario 3:** This time, you were at the bus stop in good time but the bus didn't stop and went sailing past. It wasn't even full! This time, you interpret your physical sensations as the emotion of anger.

So, our emotional experiences rely on us noticing physical changes in our bodies and giving them an appropriate emotional label. In other words, appraisal is a key feature, and it is this appraisal that explains how different people can experience the same event or physical reaction but feel different emotions. This insight led to the now-famous 'wobbly bridge' study – and explains why you should take your date to a scary film or on a white-knuckle roller coaster if you want them to fall in love with you.

The 'wobbly bridge' study

The psychologists Donald Dutton and Arthur Aron (1974) conducted a study at the Capilano Canyon in Canada, which is crossed by various bridges. One of the bridges was a rickety suspension bridge that tended to sway, tilt and wobble such that users would feel that they might be at risk of falling 230 feet into the canyon below. Another bridge was a far more solid wooden one that was only ten feet above a shallow part of the canyon below. People walking across the rickety bridge tended to be quite aroused with fear – their pulse rates would quicken, they may have sweated and their hearts would pound. Indeed, this may be why they chose that bridge. No such arousal was likely on the lower, solid bridge.

The experimenters interviewed men crossing each of the two bridges and tested how attracted they were to a female confederate on the other side of the canyon. What they found was that those men on the rickety suspension bridge were more attracted to the woman than those on the sturdy bridge. The reason given by the psychologists was that the men on the scarier bridge experienced a state of arousal that, in the presence of a woman, they interpreted as attraction for her. The men on the sturdy bridge had no such physical feelings to misinterpret.

The study shows why colleagues at work who have been through some emotional experience together (such as beating a tight deadline, winning a big contract, etc.) can end up in a romance – they misinterpret the emotions they are feeling as love!

Can our emotions really make us ill?

We have all heard of being broken-hearted, and even of people who others claim have died of a broken heart (see below), but to what degree can our emotions really influence our health?

There is a great deal of research to suggest that negative emotions such as anger, excessive sadness (depression) and stress can certainly make us ill. As these emotions increase, the hypothalamus in the brain stimulates the pituitary gland at the base of the skull, causing it to release a range of hormones that affect every part of our body in one way or another.

The main hormones are adrenaline and cortisol. Both these hormones exert their influence through the cardiovascular system (the system involving the heart) as well as other systems. Adrenaline causes the heart to beat faster and blood pressure to rise; this allows oxygen-rich blood to flow more quickly to the areas of the body that are responsible for reacting to the source of anger/stress. These areas are those that need extra energy – for example, the arms (to fight) or the legs (to flee) and the brain (to think quickly).

When we are responding to a threat that causes us to get angry, for example, an immediate reaction is required so, while blood rushes to the limbs and brain, it is diverted from less important areas of the body such as the stomach or skin; now is not the time for the body to be worrying about digestion or maintaining healthy skin. Instead, all resources are diverted to concentrating on dealing with the immediate problem. It is just like a workplace coping with a crisis; all non-essential functions are put on hold while the employees are required to deal with the immediate emergency.

All this anticipated extra activity requires extra energy, and the other important hormone here, cortisol, is responsible for this bit of the emotional reaction. The release of cortisol into the blood causes the liver to convert its emergency stores of energy (in the form of glycogen) into the more readily usable form of glucose.

This extra glucose provides the surge of energy needed to beat the source of the emotion.

The net effect of all this activity is a rapid heartbeat, breathlessness (as the lungs struggle to take in more oxygen), raised blood pressure (hypertension) and a raised body temperature (due to using more energy). All this made our angry, stressed or emotional ancestors ideally placed to deal with the sources of their emotional upset by either fighting their opponent or running away.

Nowadays, however, these responses are less useful. Rarely do we have the chance to respond to the causes of our negative emotions in the way that our body reactions were designed for. So, instead of us making use of the extra energy and resources our body has provided us with, we are left with all this emotional reaction – and nowhere to go with it. This can leave us with a range of short-term symptoms:

- **Aching limbs (arms or legs):** the build-up of glucose in the limbs can make our arms and legs feel heavy and tired. In addition, we tend to tense our muscles in preparation for flight or fight and this tension causes pain.
- **Headache:** blood supply increases to the brain, too, to enable us to think more clearly, but build-up causes headache.
- **Neck ache:** again, we tend to tense our neck muscles when stressed, causing pain.
- **Tiredness:** we feel tired because we have been burning up so much extra energy.

- **Dry mouth:** flow of saliva to the mouth is reduced.
- **Stomach problems:** blood is diverted away from the digestive system, reducing its effectiveness, and this can lead to digestive problems and discomfort.
- **Dizziness:** although we breathe more quickly when we are stressed, we tend to take more shallow breaths and thus we do not take in as much oxygen as when we are not stressed. This can lead to a slightly reduced supply to the brain, causing dizziness.

In the long term, even more serious illness can occur:

- **Hypertension (raised blood pressure):** this is the result of the heart continually working hard at pumping blood around the body extra quickly.
- **Cardiovascular disease:** the increase in blood pressure can cause physical damage to the delicate lining of some blood vessels. The point where vessels branch into two (branch points) are particularly vulnerable and, if the smooth vessel lining is torn, access to fatty acids and glucose (which is increased during the emotional response) is allowed. This causes a build-up of fatty nutrients underneath the tear in the walls of the vessels. This process gives rise to plaques lining the blood vessels. Plaques occurring in arteries supplying the heart can lead to heart attacks. If they obstruct the flow of blood to the brain, they can cause strokes.
- **Stomach ulcers:** poor digestion for long periods can result in stomach problems. In addition, there will be an excess of acid in the stomach.

- **Exhaustion:** the rapid mobilization of energy gives short-term benefits but long-term exhaustion.
- **Skin disorders:** rashes and allergies can result due to the continued decrease of blood to the skin.
- **Frequent colds or flu:** chronic emotional arousal can result in a lowered immune system, making the person more vulnerable to disease.

Broken-heart syndrome

According to media reports (Desser 2013; Wighton 2012), the widower of *Dr Who* actress Mary Tamm died of a broken heart just 12 days after his wife's death. Doctors have long known that the stress of a bereavement can trigger heart problems – studies have shown the risk of heart attack rises tenfold in the 48 hours following the death of a loved one. Broken-heart syndrome is the name given to sudden heart failure that develops after severe emotional trauma. It was first recognized in the 1990s by Japanese doctors, who named it takotsubo cardiomyopathy. It is different from a heart attack in that it is caused by a surge of hormones that impairs the ability of the heart muscle to pump rather than by a blockage in an artery. The lack of oxygenated blood reaching the rest of the body – and, indeed, the heart – causes breathlessness, pain and a loss of consciousness.

According to a study in 2005 at the Johns Hopkins University in Baltimore, any strong emotions can create the syndrome – including shock or surprise (such as winning the lottery). However, we can be reassured that it is actually very rare to die from the syndrome (which is most common in post-menopausal women); most sufferers fully recover.

2

Facial expressions and emotions

'Many facial expressions ... occur throughout the world in every human race and culture. The expressions appear to represent, in every culture, the same emotions.'

N.H. Fridja

Facial expressions are essential in social communication between humans. This is not just because we express our emotions through them (because, actually, we often don't), but because we are able to use our faces to express the emotions that we wish to – which might not be the ones we actually feel. Thus, the value of facial expressions is in their communicative role, rather than as a way to detect what emotions people are feeling (there's more on this in Chapter 5).

We thus use our faces to communicate: at the most basic level, if we like something or someone we smile; if we don't, we frown. Of course, facial expressions are rather more complex than that, and we can create quite a significant range of expressions by varying the movement of our mouths and eyes (and even our eyebrows). Most of our expressions are fairly easy to 'read' by our audience – unless we don't want them to be read, in which case we humans are quite adept at hiding how we feel (we are also very good at faking expressions, as will be discussed in Chapter 5). However, we are better at detecting what some facial expressions mean than others; a smile, for example, is instantly recognized the world over as indicating approval, whereas compassion and empathy, which are 'blended' emotions (see Chapter 1), are harder to read.

How facial expressions saved our lives

In today's world, the art of good communication is essential for business and for advancing in society.

Expressing emotions appropriately is a key part of this; few doctors would achieve much if they smiled manically when delivering bad news and few businesspeople would achieve promotion if they scowled in job interviews. Similarly, we need to be adept at reading other people's facial expressions, too, so that we can tailor our own presentation accordingly; looking serious when other people look serious, or smiling when those around us are smiling, can clearly be important social skills.

However, in our evolutionary past, using facial expressions and correctly detecting them in others was more than merely useful: it was vital to our survival. Before we had an effective verbal language, our facial expressions were the main form of communication. Knowing that someone was angry with us would have allowed us to run away before they attacked us. Similarly, showing displeasure would have allowed our ancestors to have a better chance of getting what they wanted (e.g. food or resources).

Emotional expressions that were particularly important to our ancestors were angry, fearful or anxious ones, and being able to express or read these emotions would have been essential for survival. For example, noticing that a neighbour was looking terrified would have alerted us to the danger of an approaching predator, while expressing anger showed that we were displeased and allowed others to act in order to remove the source of our displeasure. Expressing anger prevented our ancestors from having to walk away from unsatisfactory relationships; their anger allowed others to appease them and thus make the changes that fostered mutually beneficial associations (for more on anger, see Chapter 4). All of this helped ensure the survival of our genes.

Nowadays, of course, such a role is rarely required of our facial expressions, but, as mentioned earlier, they do still serve a valuable role. Reading facial expressions of emotion can be vital when trying to develop rapport, trust and affiliation; they can be useful in assessing how credible someone is, in evaluating how honest they are and in detecting deception. Being able to read people's emotional states from their facial expression provides the basis for better co-operation, negotiation and friendships. Health professionals can develop better rapport with patients, interact more humanely by displaying appropriate empathy and compassion, and make the right diagnosis by obtaining more complete information. Teachers, too, can read the emotions of their students to obtain cues about how well their lessons are progressing and how much is being understood, so they can adjust their methods accordingly and deliver learning objectives more effectively. Businesspeople who can read the emotions of others can nurture mutually beneficial associations and relationships. Product researchers can improve the information they obtain from consumers by reading consumers' emotions when they are evaluating products, giving hints as to what they truly feel – even if this is different from what they say about it. Parents, spouses, friends and everyone with an interest in building strong and constructive relationships can benefit from improving their ability to read emotions. All this evidence points to the vital role played by facial expressions even today (Matsumator and Hwang 2011).

Why do we scrunch up our nose when we feel disgust?

An evolutionary biologist walks into a bar, and the bartender asks: 'Why the long face?' 'Because it helps alter my sensory interface with the physical world,' replies the biologist (Farrelly 2008).

Facial expressions did not evolve solely as a communicative tool. That would appear to be a later function. As first noted by Charles Darwin in *The Expression of the Emotions in Man and Animals* (1872), some basic facial expressions originally served an adaptive, biological function such as regulating sensory exposure.

In the first instance, it is hypothesized that the muscles in our face evolved to adopt poses that protected us from danger. For example, we may have closed our mouth when angry to prevent us spitting or hurling inflammatory insults at our foe; the scrunched-up nose and mouth of disgust stopped us inhaling dangerous substances. Similarly, expressions of fear, hypothesized by Joshua Susskind et al. (2008), allowed the fearful person to have a subjectively larger visual field, faster eye movements and an increase in nasal volume and air velocity – all of which were designed to aid survival in the face of a predator.

These expressions later evolved a communicative function as our ancestors became more sociable.

▲ **Plate 4 from Duchenne de Boulogne's pioneering study of facial expression, *Mécanisme de la physionomie humaine* (1862).**

Why animals don't smile – or do they?

Facial expressions have generally been considered to be peculiarly unique to humans. After all, dogs can't smile – or can they? New research suggests that some animals do actually display a subtle range of emotional expressions – and that we humans have learned to read them. Dr Tina Bloom and Professor Harris Friedman, both from Walden University in Minneapolis, published a study (Bloom and Friedman 2013) in the journal *Behavioural Processes* that suggests that humans can detect a range of emotions in their canine pets and can correctly spot when the animals are happy, sad, angry, scared or even surprised and guilty. The researchers used a police dog and photographed him in situations in which they manipulated his emotions; they praised him to create 'happiness', reprimanded him for sadness, used a 'jack-in-the-box' to stimulate surprise, fed him nasty medicine to create disgust and simulated criminal behaviour to make him angry. Human volunteers were able to correctly identify the emotions, with happiness and anger being the easiest ones to spot – as, indeed, they are with humans.

It might be argued that dogs have learned to use facial expressions in order to interact better with their human owners, but they are not the only animals to communicate in this way – and other animals use facial displays to communicate with each other, not with humans. The best example of this is probably – and unsurprisingly (as they are a close relation) – primates. Research has shown that chimpanzees are capable of the full range of facial expressions that humans have, including anger, mourning and fear. However, the smile still seems to be something uniquely human, although a similar expression in chimps (baring of the teeth) is used – to display aggression, though, rather than happiness.

Universal emotions

Some emotional displays have long been thought to be universal, which means that they are recognized all over the world. The so-called facial expression universality theory has a strong history, thought by many to have begun with Darwin (1999 [1872]), though, in reality, his work followed earlier researchers, such as the Scottish anatomist Charles Bell in 1806, in this field. For an emotional expression to be truly universal, it should meet three criteria:

- The same pattern of facial movement should occur in all human groups.
- Observers in different societies should attribute the same emotion to the same expression.
- Those same facial patterns should, indeed, be manifestations of that very emotion in all human societies (Russell and Fernandez-Dols 1986).

It is thought that the universally understood facial expressions correspond to the six universal emotions discussed in Chapter 1. The psychologist Paul Ekman showed photographs of faces to people in 20 different Western cultures and 11 different isolated groups in Africa. He found that 96 per cent of Western respondents and 92 per cent of African respondents identified happy faces. Similar numbers of people could identify disgust and anger, suggesting that humans' facial displays are common across cultures for at least these three emotions. Other studies have shown that surprise achieves 'recognition' ratings of 87.5 per cent in Western cultures and slightly lower in non-Western. Sadness and

▼ **Universal emotions and their associated facial expressions**

Universal emotion	Facial expression
Happiness	The corners of the mouth are raised.
Sadness	The corners of the mouth are lowered. Eyebrows can be used, too.
Surprise	The eyebrows arch, the eyes open wide and the jaw drops slightly.
Fear	The eyebrows are raised, the eyes open and the mouth opens slightly.
Disgust	The upper lip is raised, the nose is wrinkled and the cheeks are raised.
Anger	The eyebrows are lowered, the lips pressed together firmly and the eyes may bulge.

fear show slightly lower recognition rates, but are still above 80 per cent (Russell 1994).

Research suggests that families of emotions share the same facial expression. For example, the 'unhappy' emotions, like disappointment, sadness, remorse, shame and guilt, are all thought to share the same facial display – the inner corners of the eyebrows are raised, the cheeks slightly raised and the corners of the lips pulled downward. Thus, it is not always easy to discern a person's emotional state simply by looking at their face; context and other cues are important, too.

Children learn very quickly to recognize facial expressions and can reliably reproduce identifiable emotional expressions from an early age, as demonstrated by the drawings below that my ten-year-old daughter, Elisha, produced in a 'doodle book':

▲ **Elisha's 'doodles' convey children's early aptitude for 'reading' facial expressions.**

It should be noted that more recent research, however, disputes this universality of facial expression theory, suggesting instead that there are local 'dialects' in emotional display: 'culture-specific dialects or accents would diversify basic facial expression signals across cultures, giving rise to cultural hallmarks of facial behavior' (Rachael et al. 2012). Thus, just as we speak with a local accent, we might smile with one too.

Could angrier LEGO characters be harming our kids?

As reported in the British newspaper *The Daily Mail* (2013), researchers at the University of Kent at Canterbury led by Christoph Bartneck have discovered that the faces on LEGO Minifigures are becoming increasingly angry and less happy.

The LEGO Minifigure was launched in 1975 and for 11 years the only facial expression was a happy smile. In 1989 different facial expressions began to appear. Around 4 billion Minifigures have been sold worldwide. Bartneck obtained images of all 3,655 Minifigure types manufactured by LEGO between 1975 and 2010. The 628 different heads on these figures were then shown to 264 adult participants. The participants' task was to categorize the emotions on the heads in terms of the six main human emotions, and to rate their intensity. Results showed that the faces were rated as getting angrier over time. LEGO figures nowadays most frequently feature happy or angry expressions, but since their introduction in 1975 the proportion of angry faces has been rising. The researchers expressed concern at the impact that playing with increasingly angry and conflict-focused toys will have on children's emotional development.

Is that smile genuine? It's all in the eyes

It is possible to experience emotions without any corresponding facial display – and to present a facial display without the accompanying emotion. Such hiding and faking will be covered further in Chapter 5, but research suggests that there are subtle differences between faked facial displays and real ones. We often talk of faked smiles, for example, as not reaching the eyes, and this suggestion originated in the nineteenth century when the French neuro-anatomist Guillaume-Benjamin-Amand Duchenne de Bologne (1990 [1862]) claimed that the muscle orbiting the eye (orbicularis oculi) is not engaged during faked smiles. Indeed, these assertions have proved to be correct, as more than a dozen studies have since revealed (genuine smiles are now sometimes referred to as 'Duchenne smiles').

However, smiles are not the only facial display that consists of some muscle action that is hard to fake. Anger, fear and sadness also contain muscular actions that are hard for people to deliberately perform as well as some easier ones (that can be performed voluntarily). In both surprise and disgust, there are *only* 'difficult to make' muscle actions (called 'reliable' actions by Ekman (1993), which is why these are the hardest emotions to fake. Those of us who are photographers will know this is true of surprise. How many times have we tried to capture the surprise shown by someone when faced with an unexpected treat (birthday cake, present, etc.), only to miss the fleeting moment? However much we try to get our subject to emulate that initial expression, it is never quite as convincing as capturing genuine surprise and delight.

Sometimes, we use facial expressions in the full knowledge of our audience that they are fake. This is called 'referential' expression (Ekman 1993) and might occur, for example, when we are describing a past event; we will refer to something that happened and adopt the appropriate emotional expression as a way of adding emphasis, but everyone is aware that the display is simply referring to that experienced during the event, rather than intending to be a genuine manifestation of current feeling. The 'reliable' muscles are not used in these referential expressions, but that is OK, as no one expects them to be reflecting genuine emotion. In fact, we are likely to actually want to impress upon our audience that the expression is faked in this instance; we might go to extra lengths to show this, perhaps by making our expression more fleeting or the opposite, longer lasting, than usual, or the expression may be deliberately exaggerated.

▲ A fake smile? Certain professions demand a sustained public 'face' that cannot possibly relate to experienced emotion.

How many smiles?

There are around 18 different smiles, including polite, cruel, false, self-effacing, boastful, embarrassed and so on (Eckman 2003). Each smile uses a combination of slightly different muscles and conveys a different message. But only one, of course, reflects genuine happiness; this is known as the Duchenne smile (see above). The opposite of the Duchenne smile is sometimes called the 'Pan Am' smile in honour of the American airline where flight attendants were trained to flash customers the same fake smile (Harlow 2005). Babies produce both Duchenne and non-Duchenne smiles in their first year, with Duchenne smiles being rare in the first month of life. Babies also produce what are termed 'simple smiles', 'play smiles' and 'display smiles', all of which are slightly different and appear in certain situations (Fogel and Nelson-Goens 2000).

Do we smile when we are happy or are we happy because we smile?

There is another reason why reliable muscle actions will be deliberately missed out during referential displays: research has consistently shown that arranging our face to show the appropriate emotional expression can actually lead us to genuinely feel that emotion – something that we don't necessarily want when we are recounting an event. In order for us to feel the emotion, the entire muscular pattern for the particular emotion must be used. This physiological pattern is noticed by the brain and interpreted as indicative of an emotion; my face is smiling so I must be happy, This is why, if we are recounting an emotional experience that involves referential facial displays, we sometimes end up actually feeling the emotion; for example, retelling an event that made you angry can reignite your anger all over again.

This idea – that the facial display can actually produce or enhance the emotion – was first suggested by Darwin in 1872 when he said that 'the free expression by outward signs of an emotion intensifies it' (Darwin 1999). The esteemed nineteenth-century psychologist William James (see Chapter 1) went even further by claiming that, if a person does not express an emotion, they haven't felt it at all. Although modern scientists don't go quite this far, facial expressions are thought to play a big role in how intensely we feel emotions.

In 2011 psychologists at Cardiff University in Wales found that people whose ability to frown was limited by cosmetic Botox injections were happier, on average, than people who could frown. This wasn't because the Botoxed people felt any more attractive (they checked that), which suggests that the emotional effects were not driven by any psychological boost that could have come from the Botox making them look better.

Seeing red when we're angry... or getting angry when we see red?

The phrase that we 'see red' when we are angry might actually be more accurate the other way around. Recent studies (e.g. Young et al. 2013) have shown that we are more likely to label expressions as angry ones when they are against a red background. Exposure to red, traditionally seen as a 'threat-sensitive' or aggression-inducing colour, enhances the signal strength of anger expressions so that we are more likely to view these expressions as indicating anger than we are if the background is another colour. This could even lead us to view people who wear red as being angrier – so it might be a good idea not to wear red at that important job interview!

A study reported in the journal *Psychological Science* involved researchers from the University of Kansas getting people to hold chopsticks in their mouths in such a way that they produced neutral expressions, fake smiles or Duchenne (genuine) smiles. The chopstick technique ensures that they were not aware that they were actually mimicking the muscle patterns of a smile. They then gave all the participants a stressful activity and found that those who had arranged their faces into smiles showed faster recovery from the stress than those who didn't. Those who adopted the genuine Duchenne smile recovered the quickest. This suggests that smiling can help cope with stress, even if we don't actually feel like smiling.

The effect works the opposite way, too; people who frown during an unpleasant procedure report feeling more pain than those who do not, according to a study published in May 2008 in the *Journal of Pain*. Researchers applied heat to the forearms of 29 participants, who were asked to make either unhappy, neutral or relaxed faces during the procedure. Those who exhibited negative expressions reported being in more pain than those in the other two groups. It could well be then that, in order to feel less pain, all we need to do is stop ourselves expressing it in our facial displays.

Not wearing your heart on your sleeve – why some people are 'facially inactive'

Some individuals do not show much facial expression; they rarely show their heart on their sleeve. It is difficult to know what they are feeling and, as such, Ekman (2003) terms them 'facially inactive'. This does not mean that they don't feel emotions; as we now know, feeling and expressing don't have to be related.

Some 'facially inactive' people may be so only in certain contexts (e.g. at work, where facial expressions may be discouraged) or with certain emotions (e.g. they may not display negative emotions but may display positive ones). Or the issue might be a 'threshold' one – they might need a higher threshold than other people for feeling an emotion before it will 'leak' into their facial displays.

There are also other differences between individuals. For example, there is 'latency', which is the amount of time between feeling an emotion and the facial expression appearing. Some people have larger latencies than others. People who have short latencies for anger, for example, are said to have a 'short fuse' or to be 'hot-tempered'. Then there is 'decay' time – how long it takes for an emotional expression to fade from your face. Typically, expressions last between half a second and four seconds. We sometimes describe people who maintain a negative expression for too long as 'sulky' or 'moody', or if they display a happy expression for a long time, they might be referred to as 'cheerful' or 'happy-go-lucky'.

As well as these 'macro-expressions' (which tend to involve the whole face and last for at least half a second), we sometimes display 'micro-expressions', which are far more fleeting, lasting a fraction of a second (sometimes as little as one-thirtieth of a second) (Matsumoto and Hwang 2011). These tend to be missing in faked displays, so they give another clue as to whether someone is genuinely feeling an emotion that they display (see Chapter 5 for more on faking).

How blind people learn to smile

The universality of emotions theory, give or take some cultural 'accent', suggests then that the six emotional displays are not learned. If they were learned, they would be much more culturally specific – for example, in a culture isolated from others a smile might feasibly indicate anger rather than happiness. The fact that happiness, disgust, surprise, sadness, fear and anger are recognized universally as such suggests that we have an innate ability to display these emotions without having to be taught how. This explains why blind babies smile at the same time as their seeing contemporaries.

3

Emotions and society

'The level of shyness has gone up dramatically in the last decade. I think shyness is an index of social pathology rather than a pathology of the individual.'

Philip Zimbardo

Great thinkers such as Aristotle and Charles Darwin have long recognized the pivotal role that emotions play in society. Emotion flourishes in social situations. Research shows that many emotions (such as happiness, joy and anger) are experienced more often when we are with other people than when we are alone (Planalp 1999). For example, fear might be experienced if the threat of social exclusion is felt; disapproval from others might elicit sadness; insults create anger while receiving praise or affection might stimulate joy. Some of these emotions can also occur in the absence of social situations, of course, while others seldom do.

There are generally two kinds of emotion, then: those that do not require anyone else to be involved and those that do. The former includes emotions such as happiness and sadness – emotions that do not rely on an audience or on anyone else's participation. We can be happy or sad all by ourselves and these emotions can be stimulated in the total absence of any other person. These emotions tend to be the basic and universal emotions that we have discussed in the first two chapters. We tend not to need to learn how to feel these emotions, only to learn to be aware of them or to be able to label them. Babies, for example, do not need to learn to be happy, sad, disgusted, fearful, surprised or angry – and they will feel these emotions whether or not anyone else is involved.

These basic emotions appear in the first six months of life, but not all at the same time. The order of appearance is as follows:

1 Joy, sadness, disgust

2 Anger

3 Surprise

4 Fear.

By contrast, there are other emotions that require a more social environment to be fully experienced. These so-called 'social emotions' include embarrassment, shame, jealousy and pride. In order to feel these, we need to understand our mental states and those of other people – a skill that doesn't fully develop until early adolescence. Social emotions, sometimes called 'moral emotions' because they play an important role in the development of morality, start to develop around the age of five to seven; by age seven, children can describe situations in which social emotions occur (Harris et al. 1987), but they do not become fully integrated into their sense of self until much later.

How do children learn to experience social emotions?

The fact that babies can experience basic emotions reflects the early emergence of biologically rooted emotional brain systems that include the limbic system and the brainstem. Significant advances in emotional development occur during infancy and childhood as a result of changes in neurobiological systems (including the frontal regions of the cerebral cortex) that can exert control over the more primitive limbic system. As children develop, maturation of the cerebral cortex allows a decrease in unpredictable mood swings and an increase in the self-regulation of emotion, all of which lead to development of social emotions and social emotion management skills. Caregivers play a vital role in this development because most of a newborn's emotional experience is tied in with that of his carer; he learns that his caregiver can make him happy and soothe his distress. The baby also learns that his emotions can exert great influence on those around him. This is the baby's first encounter of the role that emotions play in a world beyond himself.

Different cries for different emotions

If you are not a parent, babies' cries probably sound all the same to you. If you are a new mother or father, however, chances are that you will quickly learn to distinguish the different emotions that are associated with different sounds that your crying baby can make. There are thought to be at least three different cries:

1 **The basic cry:** this consists of rhythmic cries punctuated by rests. This cry is often associated with hunger.

2 **The pain cry:** this is a loud sudden scream often followed by breath-holding.

3 **The anger cry:** this is like the basic cry, only louder!

For parents who are still baffled as to what their baby's cry means, there is even an iPhone application to help. The Cry Translator 'involves a revolutionary technology that quickly identifies an infant's cry, based on one of five emotional or physiological states: hunger, fatigue, annoyance, stress or boredom', say the creators Pedro Barrera and Luis Meca (*The Daily Mail* 2009). The Barcelona-based creators of the app believe that these five cries are common to all babies regardless of culture or nationality. Apparently, the App has a 96-per-cent successful detection rate.

Shyness: the ultimate social emotion?

Imagine a young woman talking to a man in the street; she avoids eye contact, blushes and murmurs quietly. Is she shy? Does she suffer from a social anxiety disorder? Is she uncomfortable with what the man is saying? Or perhaps she is merely being mysteriously alluring? How we interpret such behaviour is also dependent on culture: in some cultures, such behaviour is normal and accepted, while in others it might be deemed to be a sign of severe shyness.

Shyness is the feeling of apprehension, lack of comfort or awkwardness experienced by someone who is in proximity to, approaching, or being approached by other people, especially in new situations or with strangers. There are many degrees of shyness. Stronger forms are usually referred to as 'social anxiety' or 'social phobia'. Shyness may merely be a personality trait or occur at certain stages of childhood development. The primary defining characteristic of shyness is largely a fear of what other people will think of you, which results in the person becoming scared of doing or saying what he or she wants to, out of fear of negative reactions, criticism or rejection, and simply opting to avoid social situations instead.

This, then, is probably the function of shyness as an emotion (remember that all emotions have functions): to help us develop a social conscience and to perform in pro-social ways. According to one researcher, shy children are less likely to cheat or break rules, even when they don't think they can be caught (Cain 2011).

Yet today, at least in the Western world, shyness is often seen as a hindrance for people and their development. The cause of shyness is often disputed but it has been found that fear is positively related to shyness (Eggum et al. 2009), suggesting that fearful children are much more likely to become shy as opposed to less fearful children. Shyness is most likely to occur during unfamiliar situations, though in severe cases it may hinder an individual in his or her most familiar situations and relationships as well. Shy people avoid the objects of their apprehension in order to prevent themselves from feeling uncomfortable and inept; thus, the situations remain unfamiliar and the shyness perpetuates itself. Shyness may fade with time; for example, a child who is shy towards strangers may eventually lose this trait when older and become more socially adept. This often occurs by adolescence or young adulthood (generally around the age of 13). In some cases, though, it may become an integrated, lifelong character trait.

The condition of true shyness may just involve having difficulty in knowing what to say in social situations or it may include debilitating physical manifestations of unease. Shyness usually involves a combination of both these symptoms and may be quite devastating for the sufferer. It may lead them to feel that they are boring, or to exhibit bizarre behaviour in an attempt to create interest, though this often merely serves to alienate them yet further. Behavioural traits in social situations, such as smiling, producing suitable conversational topics, assuming a relaxed posture and making good eye contact, may not be easy for a shy person. Such people might achieve such traits only with great difficulty, or they may find it impossible.

Those who are shy are often perceived more negatively in cultures that value sociability and 'people skills' (Paulhus and Morgan 1997). Shy individuals often appear distant during conversations, which may cause others to create poor impressions of them. Less shy people may be too up-front, aggressive or critical towards shy people in an attempt 'to get them out of their shell'. This may actually make a shy person feel worse, as it can draw attention to them (making them more self-conscious and uncomfortable) or cause them to think that there is something very wrong with them.

Have drug companies pathologized shyness?

Severe shyness is termed 'social anxiety disorder', though this condition was not officially recognized until 1980 when it was first categorized in the third edition of *Diagnostic and Statistical Manual of Mental Disorders* (DSM-III), the psychiatrist's bible. Since then, drug companies have invested billions to persuade us that severe shyness is indeed a medical condition that needs to be treated. But is this medicalizing of shyness simply reflecting cultural norms that favour extroversion? Perhaps shyness should be something to be celebrated because of its many benefits (see below) rather than something to be treated. After all, homosexuality was also once listed in DSM as an illness, but culture has now advanced to the extent that we now regard this as another form of normal rather than as something to be cured. Perhaps shyness needs to be more accepted in Western culture, too.

Many stereotypes about shy individuals exist in Western culture and negative peer reactions to 'shy' behaviour abound. This occurs because individualistic cultures don't value quietness and meekness, and more often reward outgoing behaviours. For example, it is often thought that shy people are less intelligent, but this is not borne out by the research. Research indicates that shy children have a harder time expressing their knowledge in social situations (which many academic curricula utilize) and, because they do not engage actively in discussions, teachers view them as less intelligent. One study revealed that, as the shyness of an individual increased, classroom performance decreased, and vice versa (Chisti, Anwar and Khan 2011). Test scores, however, prove that shyness is unrelated to actual academic knowledge (Hughes and Coplan 2010).

Being shy can have its advantages as well, according to Thomas Benton (2004). This author says that, because shy people have a tendency toward self-criticism, they are often high achievers, and not just in solitary activities like research and writing. We have already seen how shy people can be more moral, but they could also be more altruistic as they attempt to use kindness as a means of connecting with others. Susan Cain (2011) describes other benefits that shy people bring to society but which Western views devalue. She claims that without the characteristics that shy people bring to social interactions, such as sensitivity to the emotions of others, contemplation of ideas and valuable listening skills, there would be no balance in society.

Shy and great

What do Moses, Darwin, Proust and Einstein have in common? They were all shy.

Great people can be shy. Moses, described in the Bible as 'very meek', was shy, as were Charles Darwin, Marcel Proust and Albert Einstein (Cain 2011). Shy people are less likely to hospitalized as a result of an injury, have affairs (men), change relationships (women) or even be involved in car accidents (Cain 2011). Shy people are more likely to be careful and astute, and tend to learn by observing instead of by acting. Studies dating all the way back to the 1960s by the psychologists Jerome Kagan and Ellen Siegelman found that cautious, solitary children playing matching games spent more time considering all the alternatives than impulsive children did, actually using more eye movements to make decisions. Recent studies by a group of scientists at Stony Brook University (New York) and at Chinese universities using functional MRI technology have echoed this research, finding that adults with 'sitter-like' temperaments look longer at pairs of photographs with subtle differences and show more brain activity while doing so (Cain 2011). This potentially makes 'shy' people great inventors and scientists, able to study in solitude and pay careful attention to even minor details.

In earlier generations, such as the 1950s, society perceived shyness as a more socially attractive trait, especially in women. This indicates that views on shyness vary with the culture. As we have seen, in cultures that value outspokenness and overt confidence, shyness can be perceived as weakness (Coplan et al. 2012). To an unsympathetic observer, a shy individual may be perceived as cold, distant, arrogant or aloof, which can be frustrating for the shy individual. However, in other cultures, shy people may be perceived as thoughtful, intelligent, good listeners, and more likely to think before they speak (Cain 2011). Furthermore, boldness, the opposite of shyness, may cause its own problems, such as impertinence or inappropriate behaviour.

Emotions in communication

As babies quickly learn, emotions play a vital role in the social world, with a special impact on communication. Imagine trying to communicate without any emotion. Imagine delivering bad news, only to be met with a bland 'Oh, right'. Or telling someone some exciting news, only to be met with only an unenthusiastic nod of the head. We need emotional nuance to communicate how we feel, to show understanding of other people and to oil the wheels of social intercourse. 'Emotion', says one author, Sally Planalp, 'is what gives communication life' (Planalp 1999). Without emotional involvement, conversations would be flat and dull, with people acting out roles rather than being socially involved in the interaction.

This is borne out by people who are unfortunate enough to have suffered a brain injury that affects the part of their brain that processes emotions. Owing to their location, some of these emotion-processing regions of the brain, such as the frontal cortex, are especially susceptible to damage in traumatic brain injury. Such people are often left emotionless after their injury – simply unable to feel or respond emotionally. They have been described as 'detached spectators' in social life (Planalp 1999) – unable to fully engage with society when they cannot care about what is going on around them. Professor Roger Wood, a head-injury specialist at the Swansea University in Wales, describes such patients as suffering from a loss of 'emotional attachment' (cited in Newton 2010).

On the other hand, too much emotion can also disrupt communication. Many kinds of communications can elicit emotions that are strong enough to disrupt the flow of a conversation. These include accusations, insults, advice and opinions. Imagine talking to a colleague at work who insults you – it is very hard to continue that conversation without being distracted by the emotional response his or her insult has instilled in you. In fact, strong emotions can totally block communication: tears, hysterical laughter or heated rage can all interrupt and stop the flow of conversation as we confront the emotion and try to deal with it (or perhaps, even, try to pretend it isn't happening).

How TV is shaping our emotional lives

Television is there to be entertaining, and, as any producer of reality TV or chat shows knows, stronger emotions are more entertaining than mild ones. Thus, 'ordinary' people on TV are never upset – they are furious. They are never happy but are always elated. And the consequence is that viewers tend to see their exaggerated emotional reactions as the norm. This is what some experts refer to as 'tutoring' of emotions by television (Jayson 2010), whereby people think that over-reactions to

emotional events are appropriate. An outcome of this tutoring reported in *USA Today* refers to the flak President Obama took for not displaying enough anger at BP's failure to stop the oil spill in the Gulf of Mexico. He was dubbed 'No Drama Obama' and later NBC News/*Wall Street Journal* polls showed his job approval ratings down to 45 per cent (Jayson 2010).

Reality TV is the worst for showing over-reactions, especially in terms of aggressive or angry emotional responses. A study published in the *Journal of Broadcasting and Electronic Media* in 2010 found more aggressive behaviour on American reality TV than in the fictional world of dramas, comedies and soap operas. Study co-author Sarah Coyne, a professor of family life at Brigham Young University in Provo, Utah, says verbal aggression, such as insults, teasing, gossiping, social exclusion and aggression, are common on reality TV and the result of this is that 'we're setting up our culture to being over-reactive' (quoted in Jayson 2010).

Emotional contagion – how we 'catch' emotions

Have you noticed how cheerful people make you feel cheerful, too – but negative, stressed people make you feel down as well? Emotions are contagious – we 'catch' them from others and our emotions can 'infect' those around us. Interestingly, we are more likely to catch emotions from people we are closer to.

Emotional contagion happens because sharing emotions is a good way of connecting with other people. It would be inappropriate to bounce into a funeral service beaming with joy; instead, we tend to absorb the emotions of those around us. This might start off with us suppressing our true feelings and faking more appropriate ones (see Chapter 5), but before long we actually come to feel those emotions, too. This is because of the feedback from muscle groups that tell our brains what emotional display we are expressing (if we smile, we must be happy – see Chapter 2); as we subconsciously mimic the fleeting facial expressions and other emotional expressions of those around us, our brains interpret these as the genuine emotion.

Emotional contagion can be explicit or implicit. Explicit emotional contagion is when someone attempts to deliberately 'infect' others with their mood. This happens frequently in work settings, for example where someone is trying to motivate a team with infectious enthusiasm. Explicit emotional contagion can also occur by giving others a treat or reward in order to make them feel positively disposed towards you (this is one reason why manufacturers might give us free gifts to tempt us to buy their products). Implicit emotional contagion, on the other hand, is less conscious and occurs more automatically. It relies mainly on non-verbal communication, although it has been demonstrated that emotional contagion can, and does, occur via telecommunication. For example, people interacting through emails and texts can be affected by each other's emotions, without being able to perceive the non-verbal cues.

This 'ripple effect' of emotions can be prevalent in groups, where emotional mood can spread quickly through a number of people, especially where they are close to one another. This is sometimes termed 'mood convergence' and research has shown this effect in teams of nurses, accountants and even professional cricket teams (Barsade 2002). Research also suggests that it is easier to catch negative emotions than positive ones, but it is the emotional intensity or level of energy involved that really makes the difference; emotion expressed in a high-energy fashion (e.g. a loud and verbose display of anger) tends to lead to greater contagion than those of lower energy (e.g. a quiet depressed mood) (Barsade 2002). Emotional contagion of positive emotions can be a very positive force, leading to improved co-operation and decreased conflict – but contagion of negative emotions can create the opposite effect.

Emotions in virtual communication

Emoticons – those symbols in your emails and texts created using a sequence of punctuation – are commonly used as a way of indicating emotion in a medium that does not allow non-verbal emotional expression. When we speak, we can signal whether we intend a comment to be humorous, sarcastic or indicative of unhappiness by varying our facial expressions and tone of voice. The narrow emotional bandwidth of computer-mediated communication (CMC) does not allow this, so the emoticon fills that gap.

Emoticons, often referred to as 'smileys' (though these tend to mean the coloured pictograms or even animations that make up modern emoticons), are used universally, but have different accents in different parts of the world. For example, in Eastern-style emoticons, the symbols are not only the right way up but focus on the eyes, while in the West they are sideways on and the mouth is more important:

▼ Eastern and Western emoticons

Emotion	West	East
Happy	:-)	(^_^)
Sad	:-(	(;_;) or (T_T)
Surprise	:-o	(o.o)

Research has shown that these emoticons can form as valued a function in CMC as non-verbal cues do in non-CMC conversation; they have been referred to as 'non-verbal surrogates' (Derks, Bos and Grumbkow 2008). They can accurately convey emotion and can be used to ensure that a dry message is not misinterpreted in the absence of non-verbal cues.

Emoticons tend to be used more with familiar people than with strangers and they tend to be used sparingly in business settings, which is different from the way we use their real-life equivalent; we probably use non-verbal communication (NVC) as much with strangers as with friends. Unlike real NVC, emoticons are seen as a familiar, personal form of emotional communication, which suggests that more formal CMC may suffer more from lack of emotional nuance. Perhaps a different type of emoticon needs to be developed that might be considered suitable for business use and more formal settings.

Some people argue that, rather than developing more emoticons, we should ban them all, with one author complaining that 'they're the smallpox of the Internet: smoke signals on the information highway' (Wolf 2000); they waste bandwidth, have inconsistent definitions and are superfluous because a well-constructed communication should need no extra clarification. There is indeed some merit in the argument that there can be discrepancies in interpretation: for instance :-Q can mean a range of things from 'user smokes' to 'sticking out tongue'.

For more on emoticons, see: 'What Are Emoticons & Why Are They Useful?' http://www.soyouwanna.com/emoticons-useful-1264.html

4

Anger, boredom and other negative emotions

'A wonderful emotion to get things moving when one is stuck is anger.'

Mary Garden

Negative emotions like anger, boredom, jealousy, shame and guilt tend to have a bad reputation. They are apt to be seen as things we need to control, manage and quash. These are emotions that, even when we only feel them, seem to reflect character failings on our part; to express them is seen as a double failure. Yet all these emotions (like the positive emotions) serve a real purpose and, as this chapter will argue, should sometimes be regarded as heroes, not villains.

The red mist of anger

It is a rare person who does not know what it is to feel angry. In fact, according to a recent poll by the Mental Health Organization (cited in Mann 2013a), more than a quarter of people worry about just how angry they sometimes feel. Yet the red mist of rage helped our ancestors survive; anger was a motivating force that drove us to achieve the innately driven goal of survival of our DNA. Our angry ancestors were more likely to fight for food, shelter and mates than their more laid-back contemporaries; research reported in the journal *Psychological Science* in 2010 has suggested that, if we are shown angry faces, we are more motivated to want things than if we are not. If our ancestors had not got angry about others stealing their food and resources or about predators out to kill or maim, they wouldn't have taken preventative action and they wouldn't have survived.

Other studies, reported in the journal *Biological Psychiatry* in 2011, have revealed that hunger makes us angry by altering our serotonin levels. Thus, feeling angry can spur us on to desire and attain the things that are beneficial to us (like food).

Anger also helped us to work together in social groups, which brought its own benefits for survival in a hostile world. Expressing anger showed that we were displeased and allowed others to act in order to remove the source of our displeasure. Thus, expressing anger prevented our ancestors from having to walk away from unsatisfactory relationships; their anger allowed others to appease them and thus make the changes that fostered mutually beneficial associations. All of this helped ensure that our genes would endure.

Nowadays, anger still has important functions, including:

- **To get us what we want or need** Expressed anger can encourage the target of that anger to offer something that might reduce the likelihood of them suffering in any way from the angry outburst (e.g. by being attacked). In other words, Tom wants something from Fred. Fred says 'No'. Tom gets angry. Fred is afraid and says 'Yes'. Mission accomplished.
- **To prepare us for action** Anger, like stress, sends signals to all parts of our body to help us fight or flee. It energizes us to prepare us for action. Without anger, we would not be mentally and physically able to take the action that is required to right a wrong (or perceived wrong) that has been committed against us. The downside of this function of anger is that, in evolutionary terms, the action that anger prepares us for is *physical* action. Today, engaging in violence is not an appropriate response to being wronged, and we

must actually learn to override this natural instinct in order to channel it more appropriately.

- **To alert us to when our rights have been violated** Anger tells us when something has happened that is a violation or an abuse; it helps protect us from unjust or threatening action and also from any future abuse from that abuser. Thus, we can get angry only when we have some sense of entitlement or some acceptance of our rights. When these rights are violated, it is appropriate for us to get angry and part of learning to manage our anger is about understanding what our rights are and when they are being violated.

- **To motivate us to make change** Anger is a very motivating emotion and it can stimulate us to make changes in order to reduce the causes of our anger. Thus, if there are elements of our job that anger us, we might be able to make changes to our working pattern (or even look for a new job); if contact with a certain organization is what gets us going, we might switch our allegiance to a competitor.

What makes us angry?

Most sources of our anger tend to fall within a small number of themes:

- Frustrations/irritations – things that block us from doing what we want or that thwart our goals
- Abuse – when other people treat us badly or disrespect us
- Injustice – when we believe we have been treated unfairly

- Unmet expectations – when we expect something to happen and are disappointed when it does not
- Unethical behaviour – when another person behaves in an immoral way, perhaps taking advantage of someone or maybe acquiring something through dubious means
- Lack of support – feeling that other people are not supporting us or backing us up
- Lack of communication – when we are not kept informed about what is going on, kept out of the loop or otherwise not given a chance to discuss important issues
- Ongoing issues – where the same issue recurs over and over again.

How anger differs from rage, frustration and other concepts

Anger is often confused with rage, frustration and aggression. It is useful to separate these terms to help understand them and their relationship to anger.

Frustration or irritability is often a precursor to **anger**; it is the feeling we experience when we don't get what we want, when obstacles are put in our way or when someone else interferes (deliberately or not) with our attempts at achieving our goals.

Aggression, on the other hand, is the action that can result from being very angry. It is usually intended to cause physical or emotional harm to others, perhaps with verbal insults, threats, sarcasm or a raised voice.

When aggression becomes so extreme that we lose self-control, it is said that we are in a **rage**; such a person is typically very loud (perhaps shouting), may be red in the face, threatening and perhaps even physically abusive.

Do we really have anything to get angry about any more?

Mother Teresa got angry about poverty. Widespread hunger made Mahatma Gandhi angry. Martin Luther King got angry about social injustice. Yet today we seem to fly into a rage at the slightest provocation, with all manner of minor incidents set to send us into a whirl of frenzied indignation – bankers' bonuses, politicians who make relatively insignificant errors, families featured in the newspaper with ten children, fashion chains that stock only small sizes, the driver who dares to cut in front of us on the daily commute... Are these really worth the heated angst that they seem to induce? Could it be that we have nothing better to get angry about any more?

In a an article published recently in *The Reader's Digest*, I argued that, nowadays, anger rarely serves the same purpose as it used to (Mann 2013). Most of us don't know what it is like to have something to get really angry about. Few of us experience real body-weakening poverty or genuine, life-threatening injustice; we are fortunate to rarely experience the very things that the anger response was designed for – events that threaten our very existence. Anger is thus a leftover emotion, a relic of our evolutionary past. It is still there, hardwired into our amygdala but, with nothing real to get angry about, it 'misfires', leading us to get angry about the smaller, inconsequential stuff:

- 90 per cent of us admit that call centres make us angry (BBC, 24 October 2002)
- 38 per cent of us get angry with our mobile phones (2011 survey by Tealeaf)
- 50 per cent of us get so angry with our computers that we hit or attack them (*The Sunday Times Magazine*, 16 July 2006)
- 80 per cent of UK drivers claim to experience a road rage incident more than once a week (Green Flag 2007)
- Half of us have suffered from 'trolley rage', while 'changing-room rage' has now, apparently, joined the growing list of reasons why we lose our cool (*Daily Record*, 22 April 2011).

None of these triggers for our anger is life-threatening. We are losing our cool simply because we are lucky enough not to have much to get really angry about. Anger and rage are becoming routine communication strategies, instead of being the more rarely invoked survival tools of yesteryear. We are mistaking everyday frustrations and irritations for the real danger that the anger response was designed for. War is worth getting angry about, or real poverty, or gun crime, but instead we focus our rage on the man who bumps into us with a supermarket trolley.

Lighten up! Why humour can make us less angry

Introducing humour to calm down an angry person or to stop an angry situation from escalating works because humour is incompatible with the anger response. The basic premise of using humour is that we cannot feel both angry and amused at the same time. Laughter will thus replace rage. Humour can also be used to put events into perspective by interrupting the appraisal part of the anger response; when we can laugh at something, we interpret the event differently. This is why people may say 'You'll laugh about this one day', often when you cannot imagine that day ever coming. Laughing can also interrupt the anger response by providing an emotional release from the tension. Humour can also be used as a distractor – make someone laugh and they might forget why they were angry in the first place.

The physical effects of humour – and, in particular, laughter – appear similar to those of exercise, with a huge range of benefits ascribed to it over the years: it increases alertness (because of adrenaline, norepinephrine and dopamine secretions), increases respiration, muscle activity and heart rate, increases pleasure and decreases pain (because of endorphin secretion). Laughter has also been shown to be accompanied by increases in IgA, which plays an important role in the body's immune system. We look at humour and laughter again in Chapter 8.

Road rage, phone rage, trolley rage... why are we all so angry these days?

A survey carried out by the UK motoring organization Green Flag in 2007 found that 25 per cent of motorists have committed an act of road rage (*The Sunday Times Magazine* 2006). Higher levels of stress, increased cars on the road (leading to increased delays) and higher levels of impatience may be to blame.

It's not just anger on the roads that is on the increase; phone rage is also a growing problem. According to research conducted by the Mental Health Foundation (2008), we are much more likely to lose our temper when speaking on the phone than speaking to someone face to face. More than half of the people questioned admitted to losing their temper over the phone 'in the past year' alone. The problem is so widespread that the UK's Channel 4 produced a documentary on the subject, aptly entitled 'Phone Rage', in 2008.

What is it about talking on the phone that induces such rage? Part of the issue is to do with the medium – lack of facial cues, anonymity of caller and so on. Most phone rage seems to be induced when speaking to businesses that provide a service (or are meant to) – and such businesses seem to have plenty of procedures in place that seem deliberately calculated to make customers angry. Annoying music, synthetic voices and endless telephone menu options are driving call-centre customers up the wall, according to the market analyst Mintel. It found that nine out of ten people's experience of call centres had left them feeling angry and frustrated. The most common complaint was about being kept on hold, while more than half the callers said they found the music played while they were on hold annoying. The automated phone systems were another irritant but the biggest complaint about the system was that the voice did not always provide an appropriate option. Also, 30 per cent of callers said they became frustrated when their call was routed through a seemingly endless menu of options (Monk, Fellas and Ley 2004).

There is also a slightly different category of phone rage that involves either anger directed at our badly performing mobiles (cellphones) or anger directed at how other people are using their mobile phones in public spaces. A poll conducted for Tealeaf (2011) by Harris Interactive showed that when our mobiles don't perform well (e.g. they load slowly or have a poor connection), we exhibit various forms of 'mobile rage', including cursing our phone (23%), screaming at it (11%) and even throwing it (4%).

When it comes to anger directed at other phone users, there are surprising findings about what makes us see red. According to a team of British psychologists (Monk, Fellas and Ley 2004), it is not just the irritation of loud voices rambling on about people you've never heard of and don't care about that causes overhearers to lose their temper. It seems that we also feel an innate need to listen when we can only hear one side of a conversation, the researchers say. Even if it's no louder than an ordinary two-way exchange, the fact that we can only hear half the conversation means that we instinctively attempt to listen in, almost as if we're expecting to join in. It is this 'need to listen' effect that, they say, can contribute to our anger levels.

Air rage seems to be one of the fastest-growing rages and it is fairly easy to see why. UK airlines reported 1,486 significant or serious acts of air rage in a year, a 59-per-cent increase over the previous year (reported in *The Sunday Times Magazine* 2006). Reasons for this are thought to include crowded conditions, both in-flight and pre-flight (in the airport), delays, ever-more intensive and intrusive security, stress over baggage and uncomfortable environment, all coupled with high expectations.

Then there is trolley rage, which is probably symptomatic of the Facebook generation who want everything and want it now – and probably have little patience for shoppers who take a little longer over their shop. Trolley rage, however, is not only caused by impatience, but by a host of other triggers:

- General raised stress levels mean that we are more prone to 'rage' in general.
- The supermarket shop is not, for most people, a leisure activity; rather it is something that has to be squeezed into an otherwise hectic life, so time pressures add to the background of general stress.
- As in so many areas, our 'shoppers' rights' alert us to when our high expectations are not met, leading us to be angry when excellent customer service is not achieved (e.g. wrong prices, queues, checkout failure, etc.).

- Add to this mixture unintentional (or intentional) rudeness of other shoppers as they inadvertently bump trolleys, abandon their trolley in the queue while they go back for a forgotten item, steal a car-parking space or other such real or imagined 'crime', and we have a potent mix ready for exploding.

According to one source (Monk, Fellas and Ley 2004), a fifth of Britons have stormed out of a shop after queuing for less than three minutes. A third admitted raising their voice or getting angry with shop staff and 20 per cent argued with other shoppers.

For more on anger in relation to gender differences, see Chapter 7.

Boredom – an unfairly maligned emotion?

Contrary to popular wisdom, boredom is not the result of having nothing to do. Rather, boredom stems from a situation where none of the possible things that a person can realistically do appeal to the person in question. It is very hard to come up with a situation where a person's options are so limited that he or she literally can do nothing. Thus, boredom is the result of having nothing to do *that one likes* rather than nothing to do per se. Boredom is thought by some to be a distinct emotional state in which the level of stimulation is perceived as unsatisfactorily low. The lack of external stimulation leads to increased neural arousal in search of variety and failure to satisfy this leads to the experience of boredom.

▲ Walter Sickert, *Ennui* (c.1914, Tate): Traditionally, boredom has been seen as a negative emotion, leading to feelings of alienation and depression, as in Sickert's classic portrayal of a stifling and disintegrating marriage.

Like all emotions, boredom is likely to have a function. Its main purpose is most probably to alert us that all is not well and something must be done (Mann and Cadman, forthcoming). Bizarrely, perhaps, boredom is thus seen as a motivating force that makes us engage in challenge-seeking behaviour. Thus, paradoxically, boredom can be energizing. Boredom has other functions, too:

- It communicates to others our interests, values and beliefs (my being bored tells those around me that the current environment holds no appeal for me).

- It may serve as an adaptive mechanism against societal noise or information overload by allowing us to switch off from less important inputs.
- It may even serve as a 'shield against self-confrontation' (Hoover 1986, cited in Mann and Cadman) by allowing us to attribute our lack of ability at a task or lack of understanding of something to boredom ('It's not that I can't do it or don't understand it – it's just that it bores me').

As an evolutionary tool, boredom was probably invaluable, allowing us to stop attending to a stimulus that proves itself neither dangerous nor reinforcing, and turn our attention to other, more worthy stimuli.

My own research suggests that nowadays it is important to experience boredom because it can make us more creative. Working with my colleague Rebekah Cadman, I carried out an intriguing set of studies to show this (Mann and Cadman, forthcoming). We started by getting participants really bored by asking them either to read phone numbers out of a telephone directory (boring 'reading' condition), or to copy them out (boring 'writing' condition) for 15 minutes. We then gave them a range of tasks aimed at measuring their creative potential, such as divergent thinking tasks (where they had to come up with as many uses for a plastic cup) and convergent tasks (where there is a correct answer to a word-play puzzle that required lateral thinking to figure out).

We found that the number of creative answers were higher for participants who completed a boredom task followed by the creative task than for participants who completed the creative task in isolation. We also found that creativity was even higher when the boredom task involved reading rather than writing. This suggests that passive activities, like reading or attending meetings, can lead to more creativity whereas writing lessens the chance of being creative. One reason for this might be that reading affords greater opportunity for daydreaming than writing does, as shifting attention from the external situation becomes easier (Mann 2013b).

Is boredom on the increase?

Despite the ever-increasing ways in which we can entertain ourselves today, we appear to be more bored at school, at work and at play than ever before. Internet, DVDs, iPods, Xbox, Gameboy, cinema, bowling, retail parks, online chat rooms, MSN, texting – today we have so many varied ways to spend our leisure time that we should all surely never know what boredom feels like. Yet, boredom seems to be the curse of the twenty-first century, with a whole plethora of consequences: children hang out on street corners causing trouble because they are 'bored'; people become addicted to drugs or gambling or pornography because they are constantly seeking more stimulation; others take risks or seek ever-more dangerous thrills (hence the growth in 'extreme' sports) in order to relieve the tedium of their lives, while still others over-indulge in shopping or eating in order to bring much-needed stimulation into their lives.

Our rapidly changing society, with its' constant 'upgrades', 'new versions' and hi-tech wizardry, means that we have come to expect a fast-paced life brimming with constant stimulation. Moreover, when we don't get the stimulation we expect, we are ill equipped to deal with the experience in a healthy way. The boredom boom in the workplace is an especially big problem

as the growth in bureaucracy, meetings, 24/7 hours, shift work, routinization and computerization leads to boredom becoming the new 'stress' of the twenty-first century – with all its associated ills.

Embarrassment – that peculiarly human emotion

Embarrassment is one of the social emotions discussed in the last chapter and it is associated with the uniquely human display of blushing. Underlying embarrassment is the feeling of being judged unfavourably by others because we have behaved improperly. Researchers have identified three categories of situation that induce embarrassment:

1. Those to do with **one's body in public** – using the wrong gesture, wearing the wrong clothes or having an inappropriate appearance such as acne or a stained dress.
2. Those to do with **social behaviour** such as making an insensitive comment, saying something 'politically incorrect' or pronouncing a word wrongly.
3. Those to do with **matters of intellect** such as misunderstanding something or being unable to follow an intellectual discussion.

All of these threaten the self-esteem of the embarrassed person, although it should be noted that even events that ought to strengthen the self-esteem can be embarrassing; being *singled out* can cause embarrassment, even if it is for praise or an award.

Blushing – described by Charles Darwin as 'the most peculiar and the most human of all expressions' – is often the involuntary reaction to being embarrassed. Darwin points out that children blush from quite an early age, women blush more than men, people of all races blush, and that even blind people blush. However, one has to be self- and socially aware, hence his blunt (by today's standards) comment that 'idiots rarely blush' (quoted in Landsman 1996). Despite being a widespread phenomenon, blushing is little understood and seems to serve no purpose; indeed, it appears when we least want it to (and, unlike almost every other emotional expression, cannot be faked) and seems only to draw attention to our already embarrassing plight.

The blush

A blush is reddening of the cheeks and forehead caused by increased blood flow to these areas, but it can extend to the ears, neck and upper chest – the so-called 'blush region'. This differs, then, from other forms of reddening such as appear after exercise or eating a hot curry. Blushing can appear suddenly (the 'classic' blush) or spread more slowly (the 'creeping' blush). The blush seems to involve complex reactions such as sympathetic nervous system regulation and circulating chemicals such as bradykinin, histamine and nitric oxide (Crozier 2010).

If blushing is indicative of a social emotion (embarrassment), it would seem reasonable to expect that we would not blush alone or in the dark when no one can see us. Yet a recent study conducted in Germany (and reported in the fabulous *Annals of Improbable Research*) using heat-sensitive cameras showed that people do indeed blush in the dark (Wächter and Seuntjens 2013). No explanation, however, is given for this phenomenon by the researchers, other than suggesting that further research into this is needed.

So, what is the purpose of embarrassment and blushing? It is thought that embarrassment is closely related to shame and that blushing is a way to communicate our shame to others. If we can demonstrate that we are embarrassed or ashamed, then we are able to acknowledge our mistake and indicate that we apologize for it. The blush signifies that the blusher is, in fact, aware of the rules, norms and standards of society, even if momentarily it appears that these have been neglected or forgotten. This can help to deflect hostility from others who may have witnessed the faux pas. Blushing, then, communicates appeasement, a non-verbal apology or helps to put a matter right. Indeed, research shows that people who blush after having violated a social norm are viewed more positively by others than people who fail to blush (Crozier 2010).

Jealousy – the emotion we dare not admit to

Jealousy is a fundamental social emotion (see Chapter 3), and one that most people are reluctant to admit to. Jealousy is thought to differ from envy, although commonly the two terms tend to be used interchangeably: envy refers to the feeling of wanting what someone else has, while jealousy is to do with the feeling of threat of losing something of value to someone else (or having it altered). Thus, I can be envious of my friend's new smartphone, but when I get my own I might guard it jealously from my children to stop them from breaking it. A child can be jealous of any parental attention given to other siblings (because this dilutes the attention given to them) but envious of their friend's new bike.

The common experience of jealousy for many people may involve:

- fear of loss
- suspicion of or anger about a perceived betrayal
- low self-esteem and sadness over a perceived loss
- uncertainty and loneliness
- fear of losing an important person to another
- distrust.

The experience of envy involves:

- feelings of inferiority
- longing
- resentment of circumstances
- ill will towards the envied person, often accompanied by guilt about these feelings
- motivation to improve

- desire to possess the attractive rival's qualities
- disapproval of feelings.

Jealousy was no doubt originally 'designed' to protect us from losing our resources such as superior mates or dwellings.

Does Facebook bring out the green-eyed monster?

Many studies have suggested that excessive use of Facebook can elicit jealousy, especially in relationships. Facebook allows people to make information public that may, in the past, have remained fairly private – such as other people's holiday destinations and social life. We are thus all so much more aware of what others have and what we might be lacking. Within relationships, we can monitor our partners (including our ex-partners) much more closely, which can lead to 'Facebook-induced jealousy' (Muise, Christofides and Desmarais 2009). So, if you are the jealous type, you'd best disable your Facebook account!

5

Have a nice day! – emotion management and regulation

'If your emotional abilities aren't in hand, if you don't have self-awareness, if you are not able to manage your distressing emotions ... then no matter how smart you are, you are not going to get far.'

Daniel Goleman

Humans are (we assume) unique in the animal kingdom in our ability to manage and regulate our emotions and their display. Hiding what we feel and faking what we don't are important parts of our emotional life. This is especially so in the workplace, where many of us are expected to obey 'display rules' that dictate which emotional displays are appropriate. Managing what we display in this way is termed 'emotional labour' and it is this that is explored in this chapter.

All the world's a stage – display rules

We are all, as Shakespeare so famously said, social actors on the stage of life. We are rarely free to really be ourselves and, indeed, we tend to have different personae for different situations; for example, I have the work me, the me that is with good friends, the me that is with acquaintances, the psychologist me and so on. Each me is slightly different and I manage this differentiation largely through careful (though barely conscious) emotion management.

Emotion management is about the care we take in presenting the right emotional display at the right time. Humans are able to manage or control the emotions that they display by faking appropriate emotions and suppressing felt ones. How do we know what the right emotions are that we are meant to display at any given time? Our emotional displays are governed by (usually) unwritten 'display rules' that dictate the norms of expected display in any situation. These display rules vary according to the prevailing culture, and children quickly learn them. For example, the display rule 'You should smile and look happy when given a gift' ensures that children learn early on not to let their true feelings about an unwanted birthday present 'leak'; to do so earns censure from a society that expects certain emotional displays to accompany gift-giving. This process of socialization ensures that we learn display rules very quickly.

Some public display rules

- Smile when you receive a gift – whether you like it or not.
- Express joy on hearing of someone else's achievements.
- Suppress resentment if someone else is selected for a coveted position over you.
- Rein in your anger at an incompetent supermarket employee (extreme displays of anger are discouraged).
- Similarly, rein in your pleasure when hearing good news – extreme displays of happiness are also discouraged.
- Avoid displays of pride and smugness at all times.
- Look happy at weddings – especially your own.
- Suppress disgust at seeing a particularly spotty or ugly person.

Note that display rules differ from 'feeling rules'; these are 'rules' that dictate how we should feel, whereas display rules are more concerned with what we display. Thus, we are expected to feel happy at our wedding and our display is expected to reflect this. We do not, however, have to feel happy at receiving an unwanted gift, as long as we display happiness.

▲ **The funeral is the classic situation where display rules come into play.**

When display rules are flouted

The world's media was shocked by the apparent indifference shown by holidaymakers to a tragedy on the beaches of southern Italy in 2008. Two cousins, aged 12 and 13, were caught up in a dangerous riptide and drowned. What made this terrible event even more newsworthy was the reaction of other people on the beach. When the bodies were brought ashore, they were covered with a blanket, with their feet sticking out, waiting for the girls' family and the authorities. While initially a crowd of holidaymakers gathered round, before long it dispersed and everyone apparently went back to their activities – sunbathing, talking on their mobile phones, having lunch and frolicking in the water – all this just a few metres away from the bodies. Pictures of the holidaymakers enjoying their day in full view of the partly covered corpses were beamed around the world.

There are strong display and feeling rules in a tragic situation like this. When young people die, we are supposed to feel sadness, dismay and even grief, whether we know the victims or not. This is a feeling rule. At the very least, we are expected to display the appropriate emotions, such as solemnity and sadness; this is a display rule. What we're not supposed to do, however, is to just go about our business and to do so with laughter, joy and fun. The crowd violated these rules and as such, their perceived indifference caused an international outcry (reported in *The Daily Mail* 2008).

Display rules at work

Emotions at work, or at least their *display*, continue to be seen as something to be controlled or managed by employers. This 'shaping' or control can be formalized as a written set of rules, less formalized, as in protocol or expectations, or even loosely bound up with the culture of the organization. Only a limited range of emotional expression tends to be socially acceptable in the workplace; generally, organizations have the implicit rule that, while positive emotions are acceptable, negative ones are not (cited in Mann 2002).

Display rules are generally composed of 'societal norms, occupational norms and organizational norms' (Mann 2002). These rules specify the range, intensity, duration and object of emotions that are expected to be experienced – or at least *displayed*. In the case of service providers, the customer in most cultures usually has the expectation of positive affect, sometimes referred to as 'integrative emotion'. Integrative emotions, such as friendliness, are those governed by display rules oriented towards emotions that instil a sense of wellbeing, goodwill or satisfaction in customers or clients. For example, in her study of McDonald's, researcher Leidner (1991, cited in Mann 2002) found that fast-food servers were told to obey display rules that dictated being 'cheerful and polite at all times' while manicurists in a New York study were expected to display a 'caring demeanor'.

Display rules are not restricted to the customer–organization interface and researchers are beginning to recognize the importance of displaying appropriate emotions behind the front line. For instance, researchers in 1989 pointed out that employees who want to maintain good relations with each other must 'at least feign friendliness', while other researchers go as far as to suggest that emotion management is a crucial part of the role of a manager: 'managing one's own emotions, and those of employees, is as much a critical managerial function as managing markets or finances' (Mann 2002).

Cultural differences in display rules

Societal norms do vary across cultures. An example discussed by the psychologists Ashforth and Humphrey (1993, cited in Mann 2002) is the case of the opening of the first McDonald's in Moscow where staff members were trained to smile at customers. This particular norm did not exist in Moscow and customers felt that they were being laughed at by the staff. Similarly, such a norm did not exist in Israel (although recently this has been changing), where smiling at customers was viewed as a sign of inexperience; one customer in a store allegedly complained to a surly cashier that 'in America, all cashiers smile', to which the sullen employee snarled, 'So go to America.' In some Muslim cultures, smiling can be a sign of sexual interest, and therefore women are socialized not to smile at men, while a recent study into users of nail salons suggests that Korean women have lower expectations in terms of 'friendly conversation' offered by employees than white women. In Japan, smiles are seen to convey not friendliness but an acceptance that the smiler is being corrected or has realized a wrongdoing (Mann 2002).

Display rules about the expression of anger can vary across cultures, too. For example, although temper tantrums by children are strongly condemned in countries like the United States and the UK, the display rule is very different among the Yanomano people of Brazil. There, children's outbursts are seen as evidence of bravery, and so are encouraged (Mann 2002).

Studies have also shown that some cultures are more individualistic than others and that, in individualistic cultures like the UK, Canada and the United States, norms for positive emotions are more restrictive. There is considerable pressure in these countries to be happy and to express happiness. People look for happy situations, and such situations are positively evaluated. Deviations from this norm have significant consequences: unhappiness is seen as failure and, in the extreme, its expression may even be seen to warrant therapeutic input (Safdar et al. 2009). Collectivistic cultures such as Japan and China seem to be less restrictive regarding positive emotions and such emotions can even be evaluated as undesirable. For example, a study by Eid and Diener (2001, cited in Safdar et al. 2009) showed that the Chinese displayed the lowest frequency and intensity for all positive emotions, including happiness (joy), compared to Australia and United States.

Anger, contempt and disgust, which are categorized as powerful emotions, may also show different norms of expression in individualistic and collectivistic cultures. In individualistic cultures, anger is considered functional and is tolerated in the interest of self-assertion and protecting individual rights and freedom, as long as it is expressed in socially appropriate ways. The expression of anger, however, is less acceptable in collectivistic cultures because it threatens authority and harmony within relationships (Safdar et al. 2009). Because contempt and disgust are less ego-focused but have the similar ability to threaten harmony, they might also be tolerated less in collectivistic cultures.

In contrast, sadness and fear can be seen as relatively powerless emotions that lead to withdrawal from, rather than disruption of, the group, and they may thus be more acceptable in collectivistic cultures than in individualistic cultures.

The 'Have a nice day' syndrome – the hard work of hiding what we feel and faking what we don't

It would seem inevitable that people working in prescribed roles will not genuinely feel the emotion that they are expected to display all the time. To some degree or other, conflict will exist between what the individual really feels and the emotion that they are expected to display. As one staff member on a cruise liner put it, 'The company expects all employees to be cheerful, smiling and pleasant regardless of their personal feelings' (quoted in Mann 2002). It has been argued that attempting to conform to those expectations causes certain 'pernicious psychological effects' (Mann 2002). The work involved in managing emotions, by either displaying appropriate emotions or suppressing inappropriate ones, is termed 'emotional labour'.

Emotional labour in the workplace has both advantages and disadvantages for organizations and individuals.

Advantages of emotional labour

Selling more products, dealing with customers' complaints adequately (and thus ensuring repeated business), ensuring the smooth running of interactions – these are all positive outcomes associated with the performance of emotional work. Compliance with display rules facilitates task accomplishment and enhances its effectiveness. For the *individual*, emotional labour provides the actor with a prescribed set of responses and patterns of behaviour that can guide them through the often dynamic and emergent encounter. Thus, emotional labour can even increase self-efficacy – that is, the belief that one can successfully perform the task requirements – because the labourer knows how to perform the task effectively.

By fulfilling social expectations, emotional labour makes interactions more predictable and avoids embarrassing problems that might otherwise disrupt interactions. Thus, Ashforth and Humphrey (1993, cited in Mann 2002) point out that a salesperson who laughs on cue at a potential customer's weak joke is allowing the interaction to flow more smoothly than it would had they shown their real emotion and stood stony-faced. Such an actor, of course, may gain financially from his or her emotional labour performance by making the sale or, in the case of waiting staff, yielding bigger tips (Tidd and Lockard 1978, cited in Mann 2002).

From the *organization*'s perspective, theories of human memory and learning may explain why organizations whose employees display pleasant emotions (that appear genuine) may promote organizational goals. The emotional front that clients or customers associate with a particular organization may influence the decision to use the services offered by that company. Evidence from laboratory studies indicates that positive feelings about an event make it more accessible to memory and more likely to come to mind (Mann 2002). Research by Westbrook (1980, cited in Mann 2002) suggests that these findings may be generalized to organizational settings; Westbrook reported that customers who have felt good about a particular product (that is, their mood was better, they were optimistic and they expressed general life satisfaction) were more likely to remember the store the next time they considered where to shop. This could even mark the start of an operant conditioning cycle (Skinner 1953) whereby the emotions displayed are the reinforcers and patronizing that organization is the reinforced behaviour.

Disadvantages of emotional labour

Emotional labour is a double-edged sword and can have negative outcomes for both the actor and the target. For the target or perceiver of emotional labour, the emotion displayed can appear false and inauthentic. In this case, the efforts the actor has gone to can backfire. This concept is encapsulated succinctly by Thompson's (1976) comment that 'synthetic compassion can be more offensive than none at all' (cited in Mann 2003).

As far as the emotional labourer is concerned, what is good for the organization might not be so good for the employee. Intense or continuous emotional work can be stressful and exhausting because it is argued that portraying emotions that are not felt creates the strain of 'emotive dissonance'. This dissonance may cause the emotional labourer to feel false and hypocritical. Ultimately, such dissonance can lead to personal and work-related maladjustment, such as poor self-esteem, depression, cynicism and alienation from work. Other negative consequences associated with emotional labour that have been reported include general dissatisfaction, estrangement between self and true feelings, feeling robotic and unempathetic, role overload, lack of work identity, lack of openness with co-workers and, more recently, stress (see Mann 2002 for review). Ultimately, such stress symptoms do not stop with the individuals, but very much affect the organization in terms of absenteeism and high job turnover, both of which result in reduced quality of service. Moreover, 'burned-out' employees who can no longer perform effectively in interpersonal interactions are less likely to care about the impression they create, so are less likely to perform behaviours consistent with the corporate image.

Chronic emotional labour demands on employees can have even more serious consequences on health. For instance, research has shown that people who continually inhibit their emotions are more prone to disease than those who express their emotions. There have been empirical reports of an association between inhibition of anger and coronary heart disease while others have suggested that emotional inhibition may be linked to cancer onset and progression (for review, see Mann 2003).

How much emotional labour do we perform?

Emotional labour is potentially a serious issue, especially when performed chronically. My own research suggests that three-quarters of all conversations in the workplace involve some form of emotional labour, while a third involve substantial amounts of the same. Sixty per cent of all workplace communications involve suppressing felt emotion, with the most commonly suppressed emotion being anger followed by boredom and disappointment. Although we express quite a lot of emotion at work (in around 90 per cent of conversations), around a third of expressed positive emotion is faked (compared with only 10 per cent of negative emotion). In over half of the conversations I studied, people claimed that they were expressing emotions only because they were expected to (because of display rules).

How easy is it to hide our true feelings (or to fake unfelt emotions)?

There are thought to be two different methods of faking unfelt emotion or suppressing felt emotions in order to meet display rule expectations. Surface acting refers to making changes to one's external appearance – our surface – in order to match the required persona – putting on a 'face' or mask. This is all about superficial change with no change to actual feeing involved. Thus, for example, if we are required to express concern or interest that we do not feel, we can simply arrange our facial features into the appropriate expression in order to convey the corresponding emotion. In other words, we don't actually need to feel the emotion we are trying to portray.

Deep acting, however, is about modifying how we actually feel in order to match the expected emotion and outward expression of that emotion. Thus, we try to genuinely feel interested or concerned, rather than just concerning ourselves with *appearing* to do so. We might psych ourselves up to feel the required emotion, perhaps by imagining that the recipient of our display is a loved relative.

How to deep act

If performing emotional labour is an inevitable part of the work climate today, then it seems that we can protect ourselves from the worst effects of it by using deep acting rather than surface acting to accomplish it. Techniques that can be used to perform deep acting include the following:

- **Use 'emotional memory': this means trying to conjure up from your memory an event or episode corresponding to the emotion you are required to feel. So, for example, if you are trying to feel sad, remembering a funeral you attended can help you genuinely feel sadness.**

- **Use your imagination to elicit the appropriate feeling towards the other person: if they are distressed, for example, don't see them as an impersonal customer, but try to imagine how you would feel if this was your mother sitting in front of you.**

- **Method act:** deep acting is akin to professional actors employing 'method' acting to really feel what they are meant to be acting. Imagine that you are acting a role in a play or film and that you need to get 'into character' in order to perform it.

- **Put yourself in the other person's shoes:** imagine that it is you in their position – how would you feel? Try to think about the whole picture – what came before the situation, the background to the individual, their family and so on – and try to get into their skin. This helps you conjure up the appropriate empathy.

Although it has long been thought that both types of emotion management performance are likely to be detrimental to employee wellbeing, research over the past decade suggests that performing surface acting is actually more psychologically damaging than deep acting. One reason for this is that, when we are aware that we are faking it, there is a sense of dissonance, whereby our outward appearance does not match our inner feeling, which is uncomfortable. By deep acting, we are bringing our inner feelings in line with outward expression – as well as with the display rules of the organization (i.e. the emotional displays that are expected by the organization). This sense of 'match' is more satisfying and comfortable to us.

It might also be that deep acting elicits more positive responses from our audience as our emotional displays are more authentic; the negative response garnered from inauthentic surface-acted displays might increase our mental strain in a way that deep-acted displays avoid. Indeed, research has consistently shown that customers prefer more authentic displays (e.g. Mann 2002). Employees, too, seem to very much resist the idea of continually being 'fake' or 'phony', so deep acting would appear to benefit them by avoiding this label.

Does emotional intelligence really matter more than IQ?

Emotion management is part of the bigger concept of emotional intelligence (EI), a topic that has been the subject of endless debate for nearly 20 years now. Albert Einstein's IQ may have been 160, but these days, to really get ahead, many people believe that EI matters more than IQ. EI refers to all those skills that I have talked about in this chapter, such as emotion management, reading other people's emotion, and awareness of your own emotions. According to *Forbes* magazine in 2012, we would do better to focus on building our EI than our IQ. This theme was developed in Daniel Goleman's 1995 book on the topic, entitled *Emotional Intelligence: Why It Matters More Than IQ*.

Latterly, however, Goleman has modified these claims in the light of sceptics who refute the suggestion that EI really does count more than IQ. This issue was clarified by Dr Goleman a few years ago when he commented that 'in some life domains emotional intelligence seems to be more highly correlated with a positive outcome than is a measure of IQ. The domains where this can occur are "soft" – those where, e.g., emotional self-regulation or empathy may be more salient skills than are purely cognitive abilities, such as health or marital success.' He went on to note that 'in those cases where EI is more salient than IQ, the predictive power for IQ would be lower than usual' (personal communication from Goleman, cited in Mayer, Salovey and Caruso 2000). So, the answer to the question as to whether IQ really matters more than EI is: 'It depends.'

6

Thinking and feeling: the role of emotions in everyday life

'Music is an extraordinary vehicle for expressing emotion.'

Annie Lennox

Emotion has a vital role in various cognitive processes including memory, emotion, attention, decision-making and motivation. Without emotions, all these so-called 'rational' processes would be severely compromised. This chapter explains why.

How emotion influences what we remember

Emotion can have a powerful impact on memory. Numerous studies have shown that our most vivid memories tend to be of emotional events, which are likely to be recalled more often and with more clarity and detail than neutral events. For example, if I were to ask you where you were when you heard about the attacks on the World Trade Center on 9/11, you will probably be able to recall not only where you were, but who you were with and what you were doing (assuming you are old enough to remember). If, however, I were to ask you what you were doing last Thursday morning, you might struggle to remember.

This is because how we feel influences what we remember. For example, witnesses to a crime typically experience high levels of emotion – and this can affect the details that they can recall. One study of witnesses to armed robberies, for example, shows that such witnesses tend to recall the gun in great detail, but not the particulars of the perpetrator's appearance. This is because the emotion that they feel causes them to be selective in what they pay the most attention to (in this instance, the gun, obviously) and thus the details that they have paid the most attention to will be the ones most likely to be recalled. Sadly, this can make even the most involved witnesses somewhat unreliable when it comes to identification.

It is not just extreme emotions that can affect the details of an event that we later remember. A study in 2004 suggested that people experiencing negative emotions tend to focus in on specific details, while happy people take in a situation more broadly (Levine and Bluck 2004). To test their hypothesis, the researchers took advantage of an unusual situation: the televised announcement of the 1995 O.J. Simpson murder trial verdict. The event offered a unique opportunity to study the effect of different emotions on memory because a large number of people witnessed the same footage and many people experienced strong positive or negative emotions about it.

The researchers found that students who felt happy about the verdict tended to recall the entire scene better than the sad, angry or neutral students. However, the happy students also tended to make more errors of omission. Students who felt very negative (angry or sad) tended to recall less about the verdict announcement overall, but they also made fewer errors in which they recalled details that did not happen. The happier or angrier the person felt about the event, the more vivid their memory of it.

The results suggest that happiness highlights an event in memory and captures many details, including events that did not occur but seem plausible. Negative emotions tend to act by accentuating particular details at the expense of others.

Why when we feel sad we remember other things that made us sad (and get even sadder)

Sitting on a beach on a lovely warm sunny day will generally induce positive affect. At this time, we are more likely to remember other happy occasions – holidays, days out, sunny, summer days and so forth. However, when things are going badly for us at work and we feel anxious and worried, we are more likely to remember other things that have impacted negatively on us. In fact, it is hard for us to remember the good times. All of this has the effect of building on the original emotion, making us feel even happier (or even sadder).

This is because memories are linked in our brains in an emotional way. Long-term memories are influenced by the emotion experienced during learning as well as by the emotion experienced during memory retrieval. Memories are laid down by activity among a network of neurons that represents a code for the experience of, say, a day at the beach. When this network is activated by some cue, we re-experience that event – a phenomenon that we refer to as a memory. As mentioned, memories with strong emotional connections attached to them are remembered more vividly; this enhanced memory for emotional events has been attributed to interactions between the amygdala and other neural areas such as the hippocampus and prefrontal cortex (Cahill and McGaugh 1996). The amygdala is very active during emotional situations, and this activity influences the encoding and consolidation of the memory trace for the emotional event.

This explains how emotionally charged memories are stored, but how do related emotions trigger these memories? Memories are not believed to be stored in an all-or-none form but as a collection of attributes, which may include factors such as the time and place of the experience, the initial phoneme of a word, or the affective valence that a word carries. Any one of the attributes associated with the memory can be enough to trigger that memory; thus a smell can trigger a memory of an occasion when the same smell was experienced. And an emotional experience can similarly trigger events linked by the same emotional feeling.

How does music make you feel?

Indeed, it is well known that listeners use music deliberately in order to alter their emotions (e.g. to cheer themselves up), to release emotions (singing out loud with joy) or to match a currently experienced emotion (sad music when feeling sad). Research has also shown that there is high correlation between the emotions that people identify as being associated with a particular piece of music. This link between music and emotion is thus well known and accepted, but how, exactly, does music evoke such emotions in a way that speech does not?

We mostly listen to music at home when alone, doing other activities such as work/study, housework and so on. It is estimated that we experience emotions in response to music over half the time. The most frequently felt emotional responses to music are thought to be happiness, nostalgia, calmness, pleasure, love, sadness and longing. Emotional reactions to music are as likely to occur when listening at home in private or out and about in public, although we tend to experience emotions such as happiness and pleasure in social

▲ **Music can conjure intense emotions, both through the nature of the sounds themselves and the power of associated memories.**

settings and nostalgia, longing, sadness and melancholy in more solitary settings (Juslin et al. 2008).

There are a number of specific musical features that are highly associated with eliciting particular emotions in listeners (Gabrielsson and Lindström 2001):

- **Rhythm:** this is the regularly recurring pattern or beat of a song. A rough, irregular rhythm may be associated with humour or unease. A smoother, more consistent rhythm may be associated with happiness and peacefulness, while a more varied rhythm might imply joyfulness.
- **Tempo:** this is the speed or pace of a musical piece. Studies indicate an association between fast tempo and happiness or excitement (or even anger). Slow tempo is often associated with sadness or mournfulness.
- **Loudness:** loudness may be perceived as intensity, power or anger, while soft music is associated with tenderness, sadness or fear. Fast changes in loudness may connote playfulness, whereas few or no changes can indicate peace and sadness.
- **Mode:** mode in a piece (such as whether the piece is played in a major or minor key) often indicates happiness or sadness. Pieces played in a major key often convey happiness or joy, while minor tonality is associated with sadness or gloom.
- **Melody:** in melody, a wide range of notes can imply joy, whimsicality or uneasiness; a narrow range suggests tranquillity, sadness or triumph.

According to researchers (Juslin et al. 2010), there are a number of processes through which music elicits emotions in listeners:

- **Brainstem reflex:** this refers to a process whereby an emotion is induced by music because one or more of the fundamental acoustic characteristics of the music are interpreted by the brainstem to signal an important and urgent event. For example, sounds that are sudden, loud, dissonant or fast induce arousal or feelings of alertness in listeners.
- **Rhythmic entrainment:** this is where an emotion is evoked by a piece of music because a powerful, external rhythm in the music influences some internal bodily rhythm of the listener (e.g. heart rate), so that it adjusts and eventually emulates the same rhythm of the music. The adjusted heart rate can then spread to other components of emotion such as feeling, through proprioceptive feedback. This may produce an increased level of emotional arousal in the listener.
- **Evaluative conditioning:** this is when an emotion is induced by a piece of music simply because this stimulus has been paired repeatedly with other positive or negative stimuli. Thus, for instance, a particular piece of music may have occurred repeatedly together in time with a specific event that always made you happy (e.g. at a party). Over time, through repeated pairings, the music will eventually come to evoke happiness even in the absence of a party.
- **Emotional contagion:** an emotion is induced by a piece of music because the listener perceives the

emotional expression of the music and then 'mimics' this expression internally, which, by means of either peripheral feedback from muscles or a more direct activation of the relevant emotional representations in the brain, leads to an induction of the same emotion.

- **Visual imagery:** this refers to a process whereby an emotion is induced in a listener because he or she conjures up visual images (e.g., of a sunny beach) while listening to the music.
- **Episodic memory:** here an emotion is induced because the music evokes a memory of a particular event in the listener's life. This is sometimes referred to as the 'they are playing our tune' effect.
- **Musical expectancy:** emotions can be induced because a specific feature of the music violates, delays or confirms the listener's expectations about the continuation of the music. Thus, in a movie, a sudden change of pace or stopping of the music violates our expectation of what we thought would happen and thus creates an emotional reaction.

How cinema uses music to manipulate our emotions

From silent films to cartoons such as *Tom and Jerry* to films such as *Psycho* and *Jaws*, music is a widely used stimulus that evokes a variety of emotional responses. Researchers have shown that music powerfully influences the emotional ratings of faces: happy music makes happy faces seem even happier while sad music exaggerates the melancholy of a frown.

Dear God... how prayer influences our emotions

Music is just one mode through which people can manipulate their emotions. Many people manage their negative emotions through prayer. Three-quarters of Americans pray at least once a week with half praying most days, and many studies have shown that individuals use prayer to cope with negative emotions caused by suffering from illness, traumatic events or negative life events in general (Sharp 2010). Prayer, of course, can take varied forms, from simple expressions of praise, appeals or requests to formal readings or hymns (performed either in private or when part of a congregation).

How prayer impacts on our emotions is not well understood. One study (cited in Sharp 2010) found that prayer helped heart-surgery patients by bringing them a 'sense of comfort'. Others claim that prayer helps people 'calm down and decrease their fear', but all of these are more outcomes of prayer than they are explanations for how prayer achieves these effects.

The social psychologist Shane Sharp (2010) gives a novel explanation for the way prayer helps people manage their emotions. He conceptualizes prayer as an imaginary social support interaction that provides individuals with the resources they need to carry out their own emotion-management strategies. The person who is praying believes and feels that they are interacting, conversing and having some kind of a relationship with 'Someone' who can actually hear, understand and react to them. When people pray to God, they assign to the deity certain characteristics, qualities and motives – such as kindness, benevolence, mercy and so forth. The sources for these characteristics include religious socialization or traditions about the nature of God. In many ways, interactions with God are similar, then, to any social interaction and, as such, provide many of the same benefits. Unlike most social support interactions, however, this is one that is always available and does not ever bore or tire of listening. In particular, says Sharp, interactions with God through prayer provide the following benefits:

- **An opportunity to vent and express emotions such as anger to another who is perceived as loving and caring.** This can be especially important when people feel they lack real social support, or don't feel they can express their true feelings to real people. Venting can help because it is thought to take a lot of energy to inhibit anger, which is itself stressful. Thus, venting to God allows this release and thus helps the individual feel subjectively better. It is also well known that expressing negative emotions can also help us to gain a better understanding of our problems, and thus people can gain new insights from expressing their anger to God.
- **Increased self-esteem** – partly because praying is considered a 'good' thing by those who believe in God. Self-esteem is also increased because, in praying to God, individuals imagine how God perceives them and, given that they believe that God loves them, they begin to think of themselves as valued and worth caring about.

- **A feeling of protection:** prayer allows individuals to make cognitively salient their belief that 'Someone' is looking after them. This offers reassurance and thus 'calms' them down. The world can seem less frightening and dangerous when we feel protected and thus the individual feels subjectively better.
- **Distraction:** prayer allows people to distract themselves from the negative emotion-inducing stimuli that are troubling them. Thus, prayer can be a useful resource that may be used at any time and when other distractors are not available. This distraction allows individuals to stop focusing on their concerns and getting more upset by them, and instead offers a respite that can prevent further escalation of their negative feelings.

All of these benefits go some way to explaining why people who pray are healthier than those who don't, leading prayer to be coined 'the most widespread alternative therapy in America today' (Schiffman 2012).

The role of emotions in pain perception

Our ability to detect pain acts as an alarm system, protecting and guarding our bodies against potentially damaging aspects of our environment. This system is mediated by nerve fibres that innervate our skin and organs, and feed into the pain-processing pathways of the central nervous system. These fibres feed via the spinal cord to the brainstem, to the pain-generating centres of the brain, most commonly the somatosensory cortex.

Most people are aware that there is a degree of subjectivity to the experience of pain; for example, if we focus on the pain, we feel it more than if we are distracted (hence we try to distract children who are to undergo a painful procedure). Fear and anxiety are two emotions that have also been shown to have an impact on this subjective experience of pain. In a neuroimaging investigation in 2006, researchers found that those individuals who were more anxious about pain (as determined by the 'Fear of Pain Questionnaire') showed a heightened response in brain areas that encode the emotional aspects of pain, showing that their anticipatory fear could actually physically heighten their sensitivity to the painful sensation.

Other research suggests that positive mood has a significant pain-attenuating effect and negative mood increases sensitivity to experimentally induced pain. For example, in a study published in the *Proceedings of the National Academy of Sciences* (PNAS), scientists from the Université de Montréal found that negative and positive emotions have a direct impact on pain. Thirteen participants were recruited in this study to undergo small but painful electric shocks, which caused measurable knee-jerk reactions.

While the shocks were being administered, subjects were shown a succession of images that were either pleasant (e.g. summer water-skiing), unpleasant (e.g. a vicious bear) or neutral (e.g. a book). Brain reaction was simultaneously measured through functional magnetic resonance imaging (fMRI), which allowed the researchers to divide emotion-related brain activity from pain-related reactions. Results showed that seeing unpleasant pictures elicited stronger pain in subjects getting shocks than looking at pleasant pictures (cited in Nauert 2009).

All of this leads the way for alternative approaches to pain management, such as using pleasant music, movies or even odours in dentists' surgeries, hospitals and even maternity wards.

Comfort eating: why does mood have such a large impact on our eating behaviour?

It is well known that emotional states affect food consumption, in terms of both what we choose to eat and its quantity. For example, we eat more when we are feeling emotional (both happy and sad) when compared with feeling neutral (Luomala, Sirieix and Tahir 2009). We also tend to gravitate to sugary or fatty foods when we are feeling low, presumably because the taste feels good and perhaps also because of memories associated with such 'treats'. However, the sight, smell and taste of food is only half the explanation as to why we comfort-eat; research has shown that, even when these factors are eliminated (by feeding volunteers through a tube directly into their stomachs), fatty foods can make us feel happier than non-fatty (Van Oudenhove et al. 2011). Thus, the effects of food on our emotions are not necessarily due to the pleasant associations and stimulation of the tasty food, but could operate on a more biological level.

On an evolutionary basis, it made sense for us to crave foods that would help us survive famine – that is, fatty foods. It thus makes sense for the body to evolve some system whereby the stomach can send mood-enhancing signals to the brain on receipt of such fatty foods, in order to encourage us to keep eating such foodstuffs. Eating calorie-laden food has been made as rewarding as possible for us so that our ancestors would have been motivated to undertake the huge effort to obtain such food (no nipping to the supermarket in those days). Of course, now that very survival mechanism has become somewhat counter-productive, because we are still craving foods that, in times of plenty, are bad, not good, for our health.

The issue today, then, is how to resist the lure of the pleasure derived from eating unhealthy foods when our mood needs a lift? This 'First World problem' is addressed by many books and diet programmes, but, in reality, the answer is to work harder to derive pleasure and self-esteem from other sources. Of course, if it were that easy, there would be no multimillion-dollar diet industry.

7

Gender differences in emotional life

'Emotions live in the background of a man's life and the foreground of a woman's.'

Josh Coleman

Men and women are often said to be from different planets and never do they seem more different than in their emotional lives. Why don't men cry? And are women really more emotional than men? This chapter explores the different ways that men and women experience emotions in everyday life.

Do men and women experience emotions differently?

Researchers believe that the emotional wiring of the genders is fundamentally different, such that the amygdala, an almond-shaped cluster of neurons that processes experiences such as fear and aggression, hooks up to contrasting brain functions in men and women. In men, the amygdala 'talks to' brain regions that help them respond to sensors for what's going on *outside* the body, such as the visual cortex and an area that co-ordinates motor actions. In women, the amygdala communicates with brain regions that help them respond to sensors *inside* the body, such as the insular cortex and hypothalamus; areas that regulate hormones, heart rate, blood pressure, digestion and respiration (Cahill and Kilpatrick 2006).

These differences are thought to have evolved in response to the differing stressors that men and women typically experience: for women, stressors are more internal (such as the stress of childbirth), whereas, for men, the stresses are more likely to be external (such as the stress of fighting for resources). They also help explain why men and women experience and respond to emotions differently. For example, new research suggests that men and women who are trying to co-operate with each other have different feelings in response to their partner's emotions; men tend to pick up on and absorb the same emotions as their partner, whereas women are more likely to take on the opposite emotion (Randall et al. 2013). Thus, if the woman in the relationship is feeling more positive, the man will feel more positive. If she feels less positive, he will feel less positive. But, for women, when their partner is feeling positive, they will feel more negative and vice versa.

Social psychology literature on co-operation tells us that women generally tend to co-operate more, while men often try to avoid conflict. Thus, men might be subconsciously syncing their emotions with their partners' during co-operation in an effort to avoid conflict. However, in attempting to avoid conflict, it could be that his emotional display is perceived as less authentic by the woman, which makes her feel more negative:

Here's an example:

> ***Her:*** *Do you like my new dress?*
>
> ***Him:*** *Sure! It looks fine!*
>
> ***Her:*** *Humph. I'm not sure I like it any more.*

Men and women also differ in their ability to read the emotions of others. Research conducted by Boris

Schiffer, a researcher at the LWL-University Hospital in Bochum, Germany, and his colleagues, suggests that men have twice as much trouble deciphering women's emotions from images of their eyes compared with those of men (Schiffer at al. 2013). The researchers studied 22 men by using a functional magnetic resonance imaging (fMRI) scanner, which utilizes blood flow as a measure of brain activity. They then asked the men to look at pictures of pairs of eyes, half from men and half from women, and guess the emotion the people felt. The eye photographs depicted positive, neutral and negative emotions. Men took longer and had more trouble correctly guessing emotion from women's eyes than they did from men's eyes. In addition, their brains showed different activation when looking at men versus women's eyes. Furthermore, the men's amygdala – a brain region tied to emotions, empathy and fear – reacted more strongly in response to men's eyes. Other brain regions tied to emotion and behaviour didn't react as much when the men looked at women's eyes.

Men also react less intensely to emotions – and forget them faster. In an experiment at Stanford University, photographs of upsetting or traumatic images triggered greater activity in more regions of female brains than male brains. Weeks later the women remembered more detail about the pictures than the men. In similar ways, the researchers speculated, a woman may continue stewing over a row her husband has long forgotten (Hales 2005).

Big boys don't cry, do they?

The emotional differences between the genders become apparent from an early age. Gender differences in children's emotional expression have been observed as early as the preschool years, with girls being less likely to show anger, and more likely to show sadness, than boys (Chaplin, Cole and Zahn-Waxler 2005). By age one, boys have been found to make less eye contact than girls and pay more attention to moving objects like cars than to human faces (Hales 2005). Girls tend to be more likely than boys to convey submissive emotions, such as sadness and anxiety, and boys more likely than girls to be more willing to express disharmonious emotions, such as anger and laughing at another.

Socialization pressures that orient girls and boys toward different roles in life may be responsible for these differences. In many cultures, women are expected to be more relationship-oriented than men, and men are expected to be assertive and even overtly aggressive, if needed. Consistent with these roles, females may be more likely than males to express emotions that support relationships. These expected roles are reinforced and shaped in children by the way adults interact; for example, studies have found that both mothers and fathers talk less about feelings to sons than daughters, and boys' vocabularies as they grow up include fewer 'feeling' words (Hales 2005). These socialization pressures may not always be obvious or overt (e.g. sons being explicitly told that 'Big boys do not cry') but may be subtle, conveyed in the form of differential attention to boys' and girls' expressions during emotional events, attention that may subtly encourage the expression of certain emotions and discourage others. One example of this is shown by a study in which parents paid more attention to toddler boys who expressed anger than girls; the boys' anger was attended to while the girls' was more likely to be ignored (Chaplin, Cole and Zahn-Waxler 2005).

Why girls don't like maths

Although my own daughters are enthusiastic mathematicians, there is widespread belief among students, teachers and parents that girls and maths are a 'bad fit'. Only 30 per cent of university graduates in mathematics and computer science in OECD countries are female. Many reasons have been posited for this including those linked to subjective attributions of competence, but it is now thought that emotions may be an important factor. Emotions are highly relevant in learning and achievement, with anxiety being the most extensively researched in this context. Maths is thought to elicit particular anxiety in many students. Anxiety is likely to reduce motivation to study a subject, as well as changing dopamine levels in the brain and thus impacting on long-term memory. Studies have shown that girls tend to be more anxious than boys during maths tasks and that they are more likely to attribute failure in a maths task to low ability while failing to attribute success to high ability. Girls report less pride than boys after success in maths and higher indications of shame after doing badly in maths than boys do (Sladek

Nowlis 2000). These differences occur even when girls have the same competence as boys (as indicated by grade levels). Girls, then, seem to associate more anxiety and less positive emotion with respect to maths, but why?

Clearly, there must be factors other than achievement that bolster boys' emotional experiences in maths or harm girls'. One explanation could be to do with stereotypes that influence self-perceptions about maths (e.g. 'Boys are better at maths than girls'), which can lower girls' self-belief in their competence. Another explanation could be to do with the differences in the way males and females experience emotions, as set out earlier in this chapter: females experience emotions more intensely than do males, especially negative emotions. Thus, girls and boys may both experience maths-related anxiety, but this may affect girls more deeply.

Why angry women are 'emotional' (but angry men are 'assertive')

We tend to hold different attitudes towards anger depending on whether the angry person is male or female. In actual fact, men and women do not differ in how much they get angry or feel angry – but they do differ in how they express their anger. A study by researchers at Southwest Missouri State University (SMSU) (cited in Sladek Nowlis 2000) examined how men and women express their anger as well as their tendency to take action to protect or promote their own interests. Some psychologists believe assertiveness and self-promoting behaviours, historically thought of as 'masculine' traits, are related to the ability to express anger. Protecting one's rights and self-interests involves the ability to channel anger and stimulate change – for example, by verbally expressing that we are unhappy with the status quo.

The researchers found that men felt less effective when forced to hold their anger in, whereas women didn't feel nearly as bothered when they didn't express their anger directly. They also found a correlation between expressing one's anger and being assertive in men, but not in women. Thus, for men, expressing anger is seen as an effective mechanism for asserting their rights, but not for women. This could explain why women are more likely to try to suppress their anger or feel ashamed or guilty for expressing it.

A fascinating study looking at newspaper choices seems to reinforce this idea that women make more effort to calm down and suppress their anger than men. The study examined what type of newspaper articles people choose to read when they are angry and suggests that men choose articles that fuel their anger, while women choose calming stories. Men apparently read negative stories as a way to sustain their anger until their chance to get even, while women choose more positive news to help reduce their anger before a possible confrontation (World Science 2006). This is thought to be because it is deemed acceptable for men to retaliate and express their anger, but not for women, who are traditionally expected to take a more conciliatory role.

Another interesting gender difference is that anger tends to enhance masculinity for males but detract from the femininity of females. It is seen as 'manly' when men engage in fistfights or act their anger out physically (Dittman 2003). When women get very angry, they are perceived to have 'lost control', whereas men getting angry are seen to be in control and standing up for their rights. Men's anger tends to be accepted while angry

▲ Eugène Delacroix, *Medea About to Kill Her Children* (Louvre, Paris, 1838): the story of Medea, who in ancient Greek myth murders her children in a fit of jealousy and resentment, bears witness to the trangressive nature of the angry or vengeful woman.

women are judged to be less competent. This could explain why women are discouraged from expressing their anger, which can result in their emotions being misdirected in passive-aggressive strategies such as sulking or destructive gossip (Dittman 2003).

Further findings about women, men and anger

One of the largest ever studies into women's experience of anger was Phase II of the Women's Anger Study, conducted from 1993 to 1997 (cited in Thomas 2003). It concluded that anger is a somewhat confusing emotion for women, intermingled with other emotions such as hurt and disillusionment. It is generated in their most important relationships with family members, co-workers and friends. Violations of a woman's core values, beliefs or principles invoke her anger. But this anger, even when provoked, is often inhibited for fear of damaging relationships. Lack of reciprocity in relationships is a frequent trigger of a woman's anger. Cooking metaphors, such as 'simmering', 'stewing' or 'slow boil', are often used to describe women's suppressed anger, which sometimes 'leaks' bit by bit, through passive-aggressive behaviours. When anger does burst out into overt behaviour (usually after a build-up of provocation), the woman often does not feel victorious in resolving an issue, but suffers self-recrimination over what she perceives as her loss of control. After all, the woman has learned during gender role socialization that direct anger expression is unfeminine and unattractive and that anger is best expressed through indirect methods such as sulking or crying.

Using similar methodology, a study conducted over a four-year period (1997–2001) revealed key themes of men's anger (cited in Thomas 2003). A man's anger often emanates from a perceived affront to his sense of control and/or his views of right and wrong. Principles and standards about appropriate human conduct (truth, fairness, sportsmanship, professionalism) are invoked to explain angry feelings. Men also become angry when they do not have the ability to control or 'fix' things, whether the things are inanimate objects (computers, cars or boats) or work-related problems (demanding customers or incompetent co-workers). Unreasonable actions of other people that are out of the men's personal control (for example, other drivers) often provoke considerable fury since men tend to believe that human behaviour should be logical and reasonable. Withdrawal is a common tactic men use to cope with anger because, although they have been encouraged to use physically aggressive techniques in childhood to deal with anger (e.g. defending themselves against playground bullies), this reaction is no longer appropriate for adults. Men continue to have strong bodily arousal when angry but few available mechanisms to safely discharge the tension, leaving them feeling that withdrawal is the safest option.

Interestingly, men rarely seem to associate the word 'hurt' with anger as women do, and nor do they seem to cry as much when angry. Men describe anger as a rapid force that sweeps through their body while women see it more as a slower-building emotion. Men's anger seems more likely to be provoked by strangers or even inanimate objects than by those they are close to, like women, perhaps because women are evolved to care more about nurturing close relationships than men are.

What voles can tell us about love

Love is an emotion and, like all emotions, it originates in the brain (not the heart, as romantic literature would have us believe). We feel love because our brains contain specific neurochemical systems that stimulate that emotion in us. The main player is the hormone oxytocin; in the 1990s the neuro-endocrinologist Sue Carter (of the University of Illinois) injected this hormone into the brains of voles and found that they bonded more quickly with mates; blocking the production of this hormone in voles had the opposite effect, causing indiscriminate mating without any lasting attachment (Carter 1992). Several years later, Tom Insel, a former colleague of Carter's, examined the brains of prairie voles that mate for life and their less monogamous cousins, the montane voles. Insel discovered that in the monogamous voles, the oxytocin receptors were located in a dopamine-rich area of the brain called the nucleus accumbens – an area regarded as the brain's pleasure centre; in the non-monogamous voles, the oxytocin receptors were located elsewhere. Thus, in the prairie voles, oxytocin receptors were located within the reward circuitry of the brain so that behaviours associated with oxytocin release would feel good. This positive feeling associated with oxytocin was absent in the montane voles. It is no wonder, then, that the prairie voles turned out to be so committed; their brains were wired to make forming long-term attachments pleasurable.

We humans might be more like the monogamous prairie moles than their less faithful cousins. We, too, have our oxytocin receptors cited in several dopamine-rich regions of the brain, suggesting that oxytocin is also part of our own reward circuitry. However, it is not so simple as to suggest that falling in love is simply due to oxytocin release. The picture is rather more complex and researchers now think that the hormone might be responsible for the urge to seek social contact of many kinds, not just romantic love.

Either way, love is an emotion that is evolution-driven (like all emotions): it causes us to make attachments that foster the creation of new life. Love also creates attachments to that new life, so that we are motivated to nurture it even when such nurturing is a drain on our resources (as any parent of a teenager will verify).

Humour – or how to succeed on a date

Men and women are very different when it comes to humour. Laughter and humour create the strongest positive emotions of all – pleasure, happiness and joy. The prefrontal cortex in the brain, which is involved in language processing and memory, is involved in the appreciation of humour; it is also thought that the brain's reward centre, which is responsible for the rewarding feelings that follow such events as monetary gain or cocaine use, is also activated by humour. This is why we find humour so pleasurable.

Men and women differ markedly in their enjoyment of humour. For example, research conducted by Robert Provine at the University of Maryland in 1996 found that women who posted personal ads sought a partner who could make them laugh twice as often as they offered to be the source of that humour. Men, however, offered to be the provider of humour a third more than they sought it in a partner (cited in Force 2011). Similarly, while men rarely seek out a 'funny' partner, women often do. It seems that, although men and women claim to want a partner with a sense of humour, this means different things to men and to women: to women it means that they want someone to make them laugh but to men it often means that they seek someone who will laugh at their jokes.

This assertion is backed up by research conducted in 2006 in which researchers gave descriptions of potential partners to participants. Some descriptions were of people who enjoyed making other people laugh but did not enjoy other people trying to make them laugh, while other descriptions were of people who were the opposite. In all scenarios, except when it comes to choosing a friend (rather than a romantic partner), men chose women who would laugh at their jokes while women selected men who would make them laugh (cited in Force 2011).

There are thought to be strong evolutionary reasons for this gender difference. Humour might be associated with intellect and good genes and women are more likely to select potential mates who can offer strong genetic material to their offspring (cited in Force 2011). Interestingly, men find women more attractive when they laugh – perhaps because this suggests that they are interested in them. Indeed, women who are attracted to men do usually laugh more in their company – and this laughing can increase her attraction to the men. Interestingly, however, in a long-term relationship, the woman tends to take over as the main source of humour. It appears that male humour is better designed to win attention and affection, while female humour is better designed to maintain them.

Research does show that men and women are equally 'funny', although both men and women tend to laugh more at men's jokes; this seems likely to be the result of social factors rather than of any male superiority at telling jokes. Men and women do tend to enjoy different forms of humour. While women tend to share humorous stories that use puns and wordplay, as well as self-deprecating humour (interestingly, self-deprecating humour is thought to be the most attractive of all types of humour as it reduces tension and demonstrates a desire to put others at ease), men more commonly use one-liners and hostile jokes and engage in physical and active humour (e.g. slapstick). Research conducted in 2000 found that men were more likely to tease and try to use humour to show their superiority when with other men. They were found to tease significantly less, however, when in the presence of women. In mixed company, women actually teased more than men, and directed their teasing towards the men. The women became less self-deprecating in mixed company while the men laughed at themselves more – a kind of reversal of the usual gender trends with regard to humour. The researchers concluded that men minimize teasing with women out of a concern that it might be unappealing to them, while women become more assertive around men to counter feelings of vulnerability and to gain more equal footing with them.

So, if you want to impress your partner on a date, men should be witty and humorous while women should laugh a lot. But don't worry, ladies – if you are successful, the roles should be reversed once you settle down into a long-term relationship!

8

The route to happiness

'I've been happy and unhappy and I know which I prefer. When I'm happy I feel free. When I'm unhappy I feel weighed down and trapped.'

Dorothy Rowe

What would make you happy? A lottery win? A new car? Being slimmer? A bouquet of red roses?

If I were to ask people what would make them happy, I would expect the answers to be fairly predictable: money, partners, children, family, friendships, holidays and so on. But do these things really make us happy? Does more money really make us more happy? Is there a limit to how happy each of these things can make us, or is it a case of the more we have (e.g. friends, money), the happier we become? And, if this is the case, why are some people, who seem to have many of these things, so unhappy? This chapter explores these issues and attempts to provide some answers.

What makes us happy?

Researchers at the London School of Economics collated data from smartphone users via an app called Mapiness, in order to log their levels of happiness over a three-year period (Mapiness.org.uk). The app worked by sending alerts to users at random intervals, asking them how happy and relaxed they were feeling at that moment, what they were doing and whom they were with. Around 50,000 people downloaded the app, logging 3 million responses. The results were surprising. It seems that our friends make us happier than our partners – and that going for a walk, drinking alcohol and even visiting a library make us happier than spending time with our children does. And the activity that makes us happiest is sex.

At the other end of the spectrum, being ill in bed makes us most depressed. Being at work or studying also dampens our mood.

Other research into what make us happy has been carried out by the World Happiness Database in Rotterdam, which found that leading an active life is the key to happiness (cited in Harter 2013). Studies collated by the database suggest that we tend to be happier if we are in a long-term relationship, are actively engaged in politics, are active in work and in our free time, go out for dinner and have close friendships – although, interestingly, happiness does not increase with the number of friends we have.

So, does our happiness really depend on external things? None of this explains why some people who have lots of external things are unhappy while some who appear to have little are so happy. The reality is that external things are not actually as important to our long-term happiness as our internal state of mind is. The above studies that looked at friends, walks and so on were really measuring mood, not long-term happiness or satisfaction with life. Real happiness is determined by our attitude to life and the way we interpret the world around us.

One study (Kahneman et al. 2004) tracked the moods of 909 employed women. Their moods and activities were tracked by asking them to record the previous day's activities and experiences. The researchers concluded that most major life circumstances (household income, jobs benefits) correlated minimally with moment-to-moment happiness. What did correlate strongly with happiness was sleep quality and lack of susceptibility to depression.

Dan Gilbert, Harvard psychologist and host of the series *This Emotional Life*, points out two key facts about happiness:

1. **We can't be happy alone:** humans are social animals and the biggest predictor of happiness is the extent of our social relationships. People who lack social attachments are less happy than people who have them.
2. **We can't be happy all the time:** we need negative experiences to validate our happy ones. If we did not have less happy times, we would not be able to recognize our positive emotions. It is true that the bad times help us appreciate the good times.

Another researcher, the Berkeley sociologist Christine Carter, suggests that gratitude is the key to happiness (cited in pbs.org 2013). This could be achieved by keeping a 'gratitude' journal, thanking God through prayer, or just telling others what you have to be grateful for. This might give religious people the edge on happiness as they tend to express gratitude through prayer such as grace or at bedtime. Indeed, there is evidence to suggest that, in some circumstances, religious people are happier, although there may be many other reasons why this is the case (Snoep 2008).

Is money really the path to happiness?

Most people would put money at the top of their bucket list of what would make them happy. If only we earned a few more thousand a year, how happy we would be! Yet studies repeatedly show that money makes us happy only up to a point. We need money to buy the essentials in life and a few luxuries but, beyond that, more money does not necessarily equate to more happiness. Research by Gilbert (2007) suggests that having a household income below $50,000 is moderately related to happiness. A household income above $50,000 results in a diminishing correlation between money and happiness. There is some data indicating that the income threshold may be a little higher or a little lower than $50,000. This means that Americans who earn $50,000 per year are much happier than those who earn $10,000 per year, but Americans who earn $5 million per year are not much happier than those who earn $100,000 per year.

The reason for this is that the more we have the more we want. We might think that, if only we had that new smartphone that all our friends have, we would be so happy. But, once we get it, we then crave the new tablet that is all the rage. Getting that only makes us happy for a short while, before we start craving something else. Wealthy people also develop a sense of entitlement that leads only to disappointment if their expectations are not met.

Imagine you win the lottery. You are rich! Your happiness knows no bounds, and you splash out on the house, the car and the holidays. However, you soon find that you no longer fit in with your old crowd who become jealous of your new lifestyle. You will find yourself mixing with a wealthier crowd who can afford the lifestyle that you now enjoy. But, before long, you realize that there are some in the new crowd who are still richer than you are. There are some people who have an even better car, a nicer house and so on. Thus, you will still want more 'stuff'.

The hedonic treadmill hypothesis states that just as we adjust our walking or running speed to match the speed of the treadmill, we adjust our moods to match life's circumstances (Diener, Lucas and Scollon 2006). Lottery winners report being extremely happy immediately after winning the lottery. However, their happiness falls to baseline levels about two months later. Similarly, people who become paralysed from the waist down return to almost baseline levels of happiness within a few months of their misfortune (Lilienfeld et al. 2010).

However, that's not to say that money is irrelevant to happiness. Money gives us access to things that contribute to our happiness; for example, if wealth means that we can spend more time with our children, then we are likely to be happier. Or money might allow us greater social and relaxation opportunities such as tennis clubs, gyms or trips to the theatre – all of which can make us happier. Wealth also means that you can live in a safer neighbourhood and send your kids to a better school – all of which can help to contribute to our basic needs for security.

Yet it is still all comparative. What would you prefer – to earn 80,000 a year with all your friends earning 50,000, or to earn 120,000 a year with all your friends earning 150,000? Most would prefer to be the wealthiest in their 'set' rather than the poorest, even though, in absolute terms, they would be less well off.

How volunteering can make us happy

Studies suggest that volunteering is associated with lower depression, increased wellbeing, and a 22-per-cent reduction in the risk of dying (*The Huffington Post* 2013). This could be because the act of 'doing good' makes us feel good – the so-called 'helper's high'. When we engage in good deeds, we reduce our own stress – including the physiological changes that occur when we're stressed. In one study, older adults who volunteered to give a massage to infants had lowered stress hormones. In another study, students were simply asked to watch a film of Mother Teresa's work with the poor in Calcutta. They had significant increases in protective antibodies associated with improved immunity – and antibody levels remained high for an hour afterwards. Students who watched a more neutral film didn't have changes in their antibody levels. This shows that even witnessing good deeds can make us feel better (Lerche Davis 2005).

However, it isn't just the stress-reducing properties of doing good deeds that create the 'helper's high'. Using MRI scans, scientists have identified specific regions of the brain that are very active during deeply empathic and compassionate emotions. These brain studies show that this creates a state of joy and delight that comes from giving to others. A recent study has identified high levels of the 'bonding' hormone oxytocin in people who are very generous towards others (Lerche Davis 2005).

Ha ha! – the benefits of laughter

Laughter is thought to be a powerful stress reducer. Research shows that people with a good sense of humour may not experience less stress, but are better able to cope with it (Moran and Massam 1997). For example, a study of occupational therapists showed that using humour as part of stress management can provide effective personal coping mechanisms for the therapists (Vergeer and MacRae 1993).

Humour releases tension – it is very difficult to enjoy humour while being stressed. This is why a sign of chronic stress is when individuals no longer find humour or fun in life any more and why humour can be an effective form of stress management (McGhee 2011). Indeed, the physical effects of humour (in particular, laughter) appear similar to those of exercise, with a huge range of benefits ascribed to it over the years: increased alertness (because of adrenaline, norepinephrine and dopamine secretions), increased respiration, increased muscle activity and heart rate, increased pleasure and decreased pain (because of endorphin secretion). Laughter has also been shown to be accompanied by increasing levels of IgA, which is an important part of the immune system (Moran and Massam 1997). All of this goes to explain why, when someone is sad or upset, we try to make them laugh so that they feel better; if we can get them to laugh, endorphins are released that lift their mood.

Why do humans laugh? (And do other animals laugh too?)

Laughter can be regarded as an 'extreme smile' – a smile with accompanying vocal sounds. It emerges early in human development (though later than smiling alone), being reliably elicited through tickling by about four months of age (Bachorowshi and Owren 2004). Children born both deaf and blind also laugh at roughly the same age, indicating that this behaviour is innate. Although sometimes regarded as a stereotyped action, meaning that it tends to be constant in form, researchers have instead found laughter to be remarkably variable. In fact, laughter may be better thought of as a broad class of sounds with relatively distinct subtypes, each of which may function somewhat differently in a social interaction.

In order to characterize the acoustic features of laughter, researchers analysed over a thousand laughs that were produced by 97 college students as they watched two humorous film clips (Bachorowshi and Owren 2004).

The first finding of import was that laugh sounds can be readily grouped into voiced and unvoiced varieties. Voiced laughter means that there are regular vibrations of the vocal folds during production, giving the sound a tonal, vowel-like quality. Voiced laughs are the versions that are commonly thought of as typical laughter. Unvoiced laughs can be very similar to voiced versions, but lack regular vocal-fold vibration. This makes them noisy and atonal in comparison, and they include sounds that can be described as grunt-like or snort-like. Many laughs consist of a mix of voiced and unvoiced components. In the study, males produced more grunt-like laughs than females, whereas females produced more voiced laughs than did the males.

Laughter does not often occur without a social context – we rarely laugh alone. In fact, we are 30 times more likely to laugh in the presence of others than when we are alone (Blaine, Greteman and Odewire 2009). Both smiling and laughing are thus part of the social repertoire that our ancestors developed when they started to mix in larger groups, to help them form and maintain positive and co-operative relationships with others. Laughter 'works' not because it vocalizes a state of positive emotion, but by inducing positive affective responses in listeners. This emotion-inducing effect thereby primes listeners to behave positively towards laughers. Laughing is thus a subconscious strategy of social influence (Bachorowshi and Owren 2004).

Of course, it should be noted that humans are not unique in being able to laugh. Our closest mammalian ancestors – apes and chimpanzees – both laugh, though probably not at the same things we do. When apes play, they roughhouse, tickle and laugh, although few of us would mistake an ape's cackle for the human equivalent (Blaine, Greteman and Odewire 2009).

Some facts about laughter

- Speakers laugh more than listeners.
- Women laugh more than men.
- Laughter punctuates our phrases but doesn't usually interrupt them.
- Laughter is contagious.
- For couples, the absence of laughter predicts divorce far more consistently than the presence of outright animosity.
- There are 40 to 50 qualitatively distinct kinds of laughs with distinct meanings (Blaine, Greteman and Odewire 2009).

The black dog of depression

Most people know what it is to feel down or depressed at times. Depression is not simply the opposite of happiness because, when we are unhappy, others can cheer us up or offer us comfort (and we can even seek out such comfort ourselves). When we are depressed, however, no one can reach us, and we are certainly unable to lift ourselves out of its depths.

According to the World Health Organization, depression affects just over 120 million people worldwide with about a fifth of the world's population experiencing the 'black dog' at any one time (Watts 2012). There are four main groups of depressive symptoms:

1 Those to do with **feelings** (e.g. feeling sad and miserable)
2 **Physical symptoms** (e.g. lack of appetite or sleeping difficulties)
3 **Thoughts/cognitions** (e.g. 'I am worthless', 'No one likes me')
4 Those to do with **behaviour** (e.g. staying in bed).

It is a myth to believe that depression is much more common among women than men. A study published in *JAMA Psychiatry* (August 2013 issue) showed that depression affects 30.6 per cent of men and 33.3 per cent of women, not a statistically significant difference.

Origins of the 'black dog'

Many people assume that Winston Churchill coined the term when he was describing his own depression, but he was in fact quoting his nanny when he referred to his 'black dog'. Apparently, English nannies of the time used to accuse their grumpy charges of 'having a black dog on your back'.

If, as was explained in Chapter 1, all emotions have an adaptive purpose, what, then, is the point of such excessive sadness? Studies show that, when we are sad, we think in a more systematic manner. Sad people are attentive to details and externally oriented, while happy people tend to make snap judgements. This suggests, then, that sadness can be good for us. Indeed, it could be argued that some unhappiness is useful, if only so that we can appreciate the good times (Gilbert 2007).

Depression, of course, is more than just sadness. It is an extreme version of that emotion and is so debilitating that it can threaten to take over and seriously inhibit normal functioning. So how does a depressed person find the path to happiness again? Although antidepressants can be life-saving for some individuals, initial drug therapy produces full benefits in only 30 to 40 per cent of patients. Even after trying two to four different drugs, one-third of people will remain depressed (figures cited in Layous et al. 2011).

According to a study published in 2011, 'positive activity interventions' (PAIs) are the real key to treating depression (Layous et al. 2011). PAIs are intentional activities such as performing acts of kindness, practising optimism and counting one's blessings – activities gleaned from decades of research into how happy and unhappy people are different. PAIs may act to boost the dampened reward/ pleasure circuit mechanisms and reverse apathy – a key benefit that does not usually arise from treatment with medication alone. There can be long-term benefits of practising even such brief, positive activities. For example, if a person gets 15 minutes of positive emotions from counting her blessings, she may muster the energy to attend the art class she'd long considered attending, and, while in class, might meet a friend who becomes a companion and confidant for years to come. In this way, even short-lived positive feelings can lead to long-term social, psychological and intellectual benefits .

Why do some people never get depressed?

Marriage breakdown, bereavement, redundancy... any one of these life events would surely be enough to spark depression in anyone. Yet this is not the case – some people manage to stay buoyant and cheerful in the face of severe adversity, whereas others fall apart at the first signs of trouble. Why is that?

Psychologists believe that the answer lies in the phenomenon of resiliency. Psychological resilience is an individual's ability to cope with stress and adversity. This coping may result in the individual 'bouncing back' quickly from being unhappy, or simply not getting too upset in the first place. Resilience is thought to be tied in with cognitive flexibility – our capacity to adapt our thinking to different situations – and to the extent to which our brains concentrate on processing and remembering happy, as opposed to sad, information (emotional memory). Many studies show that the primary factor is to have relationships that provide care and support, create love and trust and offer encouragement, both within and outside the family. Other factors that can increase resilience are the ability to make plans and having self-confidence and a positive self-image.

This 100 ideas section gives ways you can explore the subject in more depth. It's much more than just the usual reading list.

100 IDEAS

Seven great quotes about emotions

1 'Emotions help humans solve many of the basic problems of social living.' (Keltner and Haidt 2001)

2 'Emotions contain the wisdom of the ages.' (Lazarus 1991)

3 'A world without any affect would be a pallid, meaningless world. We would know that things happened, but we could not care whether they did or not.' (Tomkins 1979)

4 'The best and most beautiful things in the world cannot be seen or even touched. They must be felt with the heart.' Helen Keller, US deafblind activist (1880–1968)

5 'I don't want to be at the mercy of my emotions. I want to use them, to enjoy them, and to dominate them.' Dorian Gray, in Oscar Wilde, *The Picture of Dorian Gray* (1890)

6 'Do not let another day go by where your dedication to other people's opinions is greater than your dedication to your own emotions!' Steve Maraboli, *Life, the Truth, and Being Free* (2009)

7 'When dealing with people, remember you are not dealing with creatures of logic, but creatures of emotion.' Dale Carnegie, US writer (1888–1955)

Three quotes about facial expressions

8 'The young and the old of widely different races, both with man and animals, express the same state of mind by the same movements.' Charles Darwin, *The Expression of the Emotions in Man and Animals* (1872)

9 'Everyone knows that grief involves a gloomy and joy a cheerful countenance. ... There are characteristic facial expressions which are observed to accompany anger, fear, erotic excitement, and all the other passions.' Corpus Aristotelicum, *Physiognomonica* (300 BCE)

10 'There is a face beneath this mask, but it isn't me. I'm no more that face than I am the muscles beneath it, or the bones beneath that.' 'V', in Alan Moore, *V for Vendetta* (1982–89)

Six curious facts about emotions

11 Ancient doctors believed that **different organs controlled certain moods.** Happiness, for example, came from the heart, anger from the liver and fear from the kidneys.

12 In the English language, there are **more than 400 words** assigned to emotions and sentiments.

13 A recent study (Rheyanne 2012) suggests **a strong correlation between wearing certain clothes and**

emotional states. For example, it revealed that women who are depressed or sad are more likely to wear baggy tops, sweatshirts or jeans. Women who had more positive emotions were more likely to wear a favourite dress or jewellery.

14 **The word 'emotion'** derives from the Latin *emovere*, 'to move out, remove, agitate'.

15 **Colours can profoundly affect emotional responses.** While not everyone experiences the same emotion in response to a particular colour, most people find reds and oranges stimulating and blues and purples restful. In contrast, grey, brown, black and white tend to be emotionally dulling. In fact, studies reveal that children playing in an orange room were friendlier, more alert and creative and less irritable than children in playrooms painted white, brown and black (MacDonald 2008).

16 A human can make **over 10,000 facial expressions** to express a wide variety of subtle emotions (Ekman 2003).

Six books about emotion

17 Sally Planalp, *Communicating Emotion: Social, Moral, and Cultural Processes* (Cambridge University Press, 1999)

18 Sandi Mann, *Hiding What We Feel, Faking What We Don't: Understanding the Role of Your Emotions at Work* (Element Books, 1999)

19 Paul Ekman, *Emotions Revealed: Understanding Faces and Feelings* (Phoenix, 2004)

20 Paul Seager and Sandi Mann, *Would I Lie to You? Deception Detection in Relationships at Work and in Life* (Albert Bridge Books, 2013)

21 Dacher Keltner, Keith Oatley and Jennifer M. Jenkins, *Understanding Emotions* (John Wiley and Sons, 2006)

22 Michael Lewis, Jeannette M. Haviland-Jones and Lisa Feldman Barrett, *Handbook of Emotions* (Guildford Press 2010)

Five books about emotions for younger children

23 Brian Moses (author) and Mike Gordon (illustrator), *I Feel Angry* (Your Emotions) (Wayland, 1994)

24 Brian Moses (author) and Mike Gordon (illustrator), *I Feel Sad* (Your Emotions) (Wayland, 1994)

25 Brian Moses (author) and Mike Gordon (illustrator), *I'm Worried* (Your Emotions) (Wayland, 1994)

26 Brian Moses (author) and Mike Gordon (illustrator), *I Feel Jealous* (Your Emotions) (Wayland, 1994)

27 Cheri J. Meiners (author) and Meredith Johnson (illustrator), *Cool Down and Work through Anger* (Learning to Get Along) (Free Spirit Publishing, 2010)

Two great happiness projects

28 Action for Happiness http://www.actionforhappiness.org/

29 The Happiness Project http://www.happiness-project.com/

Ten ways to be happy

(From Action for Happiness – www.happinessproject.org – with permission)

30 **Giving** Do things for others

31 **Relating** Connect with people

32 **Exercising** Take care of your body

33 **Appreciating** Notice the world around you

34 **Trying out** Keep learning new things

35 **Direction** Have goals to look forward to

36 **Resilience** Find ways to bounce back

37 **Emotion** Take a positive approach

38 **Acceptance** Be comfortable with who you are

39 **Meaning** Be part of something bigger

Two YouTube films to watch about depression

40 World Health Organization video about depression http://www.youtube.com/watch?v=XiCrniLQGYc

41 UK writer, actor and presenter Stephen Fry on manic depression (bipolar) http://www.youtube.com/watch?v=cKiAz6ndUbU

Ten tips to beat depression

(Based on Sandi Mann, *Overcoming Panic Attacks and Phobias* (Hodder & Stoughton, 2013))

42 Focus on the here and now, not the future or the past.

43 Look for simple pleasures in everyday life.

44 Do some gentle exercise every day.

45 Eat healthy food.

46 Sleep only at night.

47 Take things one step at a time.

48 Take up interests or hobbies, even if you don't think you will enjoy them.

49 Be kind to yourself.

50 Do voluntary work.

51 Do something nice for someone else.

Five books about depression

52 Paul Gilbert, *Overcoming Depression: A Self-help Guide Using Cognitive Behavioural Techniques* (Robinson, 2009)

53 Steve Ilardi, *Depression Cure: The Six-step Programme to Beat Depression without Drugs* (Vermilion, 2010)

54 Mark William, John Teasdale, Zindel Segal and Jon Kabat-Zinn, *The Mindful Way through Depression: Freeing Yourself from Chronic Unhappiness* (Guildford Press, 2007)

55 Gwyneth Lewis, *Sunbathing in the Rain: A Cheerful Book about Depression* (Harper Perennial, 2006)

56 Dorothy Rowe, *Depression: The Way Out of Your Prison* (Routledge, 2003)

Five ways to reduce your anger

(taken from Sandi Mann, *Manage Your Anger* (Hodder & Stoughton, 2013))

57 **Reduce your general stress levels** by looking at stress management techniques.

58 **Lower your expectations** about how perfect life should be.

59 Accept that things **don't always go according to plan** in life.

60 Take time out while you simmer down in order to **view the incident from a different perspective.**

61 **Don't take things personally** or see affronts as personal attacks.

Five great newspaper features about emotions

62 Sandra Blakeslee, 'Tracing the Brain's Pathways for Linking Emotion and Reason', *International New York Times* (6 December 1994) http://www.nytimes.com/1994/12/06/science/tracing-the-brain-s-pathways-for-linking-emotion-and-reason.html?pagewanted=all&src=pm

63 Luisa Dillner, 'Should I be more emotional?' *The Guardian* (15 September 2013) http://www.theguardian.com/lifeandstyle/2013/sep/15/should-i-be-more-emotional

64 Sandi Mann, 'Why are we all so angry these days?' *Huffington Post* (25 January 2013) http://www.huffingtonpost.co.uk/sandi-mann/why-are-we-all-so-angry-these-days_b_2540474.html?utm_hp_ref=uk

65 Susie Mesure and Amy Lewin, 'The Difficult Princesses: Animating female characters is harder, says Disney boss, because of their "range of emotions"', *The Independent on Sunday*, 13 October 2013 http://www.independent.co.uk/arts-entertainment/films/news/the-difficult-princesses-animating-female-characters-is-harder-says-disney-boss-because-of-their-range-of-emotions-8876499.html

One great song for children about emotions

66 'The Emotion Song' by Debbie Doo and Friends http://www.youtube.com/watch?v=7AkKk8XIcgU

...and one great web-based game

67 BBC CBeebies, Tikkabilla Emotion Theatre http://www.bbc.co.uk/cbeebies/tikkabilla/games/tikkabilla-emotiontheatre

Thirteen people who were (arguably) the greatest influences on our understanding of emotion

68 Paul Ekman

69 Daniel Goleman

70 Robert Plutchik

71 Charles Darwin

72 William James

73 John Cacippio

74 Carl Lange

75 Walter Cannon

76 Phillip Bard

77 Stanley Schachter

78 Jerome Singer

79 Richard Lazarus

80 Arlie Russell Hochschild

Three great quotes about love

81 'You know you're in love when you can't fall asleep because reality is finally better than your dreams.' Dr Seuss

82 'Love is that condition in which the happiness of another person is essential to your own.' Robert A. Heinlein, *Stranger in a Strange Land* (1961)

83 'Where there is love there is life.' Mahatma Gandhi

Five books about jealousy

84 Paul A. Hauck, *Jealousy: Why it Happens and How to Overcome It* (Sheldon Press, 1993)

85 Dr Windy Dryden, *Overcoming Jealousy* (Overcoming Common Problems) (Sheldon Press, 2005)

86 Kelly White, *Jealousy: How to Kill It Before It Kills Your Relationship* (Kindle)

87 Lynda Bevan, *Life without Jealousy: A Practical Guide* (10-Step Empowerment Series) (Loving Healing Press, 2009)

88 Rebecca Steel, *How to Overcome Jealousy: How to Stop Jealousy Dead in Its Tracks* (CreateSpace Independent Publishing Platform, 2011)

Four quotes about jealousy from the Bible

89 **James 3:16:** 'For where jealousy and selfish ambition exist, there will be disorder and every vile practice.'

90 **Exodus 20:17:** 'You shall not covet your neighbour's house; you shall not covet your neighbour's wife, or his male servant, or his female servant, or his ox, or his donkey, or anything that is your neighbour's.'

91 **Deuteronomy 4:24:** 'For the Lord your God is a consuming fire, a jealous God.'

92 **Proverbs 14:30:** 'A tranquil heart gives life to the flesh, but envy makes the bones rot.'

One resource on emoticons

93 M. Osterhoudt, *The Dictionary of Emoticons: No Words Allowed* (Kindle)

Two books about disgust

94 Susan B. Miller, *Disgust: The Gatekeeper Emotion* (Routledge, 2004)

95 Valerie Curtis, *Don't Look, Don't Touch: The Science behind Revulsion* (Oxford University Press, 2013)

Two interesting resources about embarrassment and blushing

96 Nick Collins, 'Blushing in the Dark: First Experimental Proof', *The Telegraph* (4 September 2013) http://www.telegraph.co.uk/science/science-news/10285883/Blushing-in-the-dark-first-experimental-proof.html

97 Robert J. Edelmann, *Coping with Blushing* (Overcoming Common Problems) (Sheldon Press, 2004)

Three inspiring quotes about emotions from the Bible

98 **Proverbs 29:11:** 'A fool gives full vent to his spirit, but a wise man quietly holds it back.'

99 **Romans 12:15:** 'Rejoice with those who rejoice, weep with those who weep.'

100 **Romans 12:9:** 'Let love be genuine. Abhor what is evil; hold fast to what is good.'

References

Chapter 1

Desser, R. 'Yes, you can die from a broken heart'. http://abcnews.go.com/blogs/health/2013/02/14/yes-you-can-die-from-a-broken-heart/

Dutton, D.G., and Aron, A.P. (1974). 'Some evidence for heightened sexual attraction under conditions of high anxiety'. *Journal of Personality and Social Psychology* 30: 510–17.

Ekman, P. (1992). 'An argument for basic emotions'. *Cognition & Emotion* 6: 169–200.

Landman, J. (1996). 'Social control of "negative" emotions: the case of regret'. In R. Harré and W.G. Parrott (eds), *The Emotions: Social, Cultural and Biological Dimensions.* London: Sage Publications, 1996.

Plutchik, R. (2002). 'Nature of emotions'. *American Scientist* 89: 349.

Schachter, S., and Singer, J. (1962). 'Cognitive, social, and physiological determinants of emotional state'. *Psychological Review* 69: 379–99.

Wighton, K. (2012). 'You really can die of a broken heart – however healthy you are'. *Daily Mail*, 13 August.

Chapter 2

Bloom, T., and Friedman, H. 'Classifying dogs' (*Canis familiaris*) facial expressions from photographs'. *Behavioural Processes* 96 (June): 1–10.

Daily Mail (2013). 'Lego characters are getting angrier – and could be harming children's development'. *Daily Mail*, 12 June 2013.

Darwin, C. (1999 [1872]). *The Expression of the Emotions in Man and Animals.* London: Fontana Press.

Duchenne de Boulogne, G.-B. (1990 [1862]). *The Mechanism of Human Facial Expression*, trans. R.A. Cuthbertson. Cambridge: Cambride University Press.

Ekman, P. (1993). 'Facial expression and emotion'. *American Psychologist* 48(4): 384–92.

Ekman, P. (2003) *Emotions Revealed.* New York, NY: Henry Holt and Company.

Farrelly, C. (2008). http://colinfarrelly.blogspot.co.uk/2008/07/evolution-of-facial-expressions.html

Fogel, A., and Nelson-Goens, G.C. (2000). 'Do different infant smiles reflect different positive emotuions?' *Social Development* 9(4): 497–520.

Frijda, N.H. (1986). *The Emotions.* Cambridge: Cambridge University Press.

Harlow, J. (2005). 'The smile that says where you're from'. *The Sunday Times*, 20 February 20.

Matsumoto, D., and Hwang, H.S. (2011). 'Reading facial expressions of emotion'. *Psychological Science Agenda* (May 2011).

Rachael, E.J., et al. (2012). 'Facial expressions of emotion are not culturally universal', *Proceedings of the National Society of Sciences of the United States of America*.

Russell, J.A. (1994), 'Is there universal recognition of emotion from facial expression? A review of the cross-cultural studies'. *Psychological Bulletin* 115/1: 102–41.

Russell, J.A., and Fernandez-Dols, J.M. (1998). 'What does a facial expression mean?' In J.M. Jenkins, K. Oakley and N. Stein (eds). *Human Emotions: A Reader* (Wiley-Blackwell), pp. 73–8.

Susskind, J.M., et al. (2008). 'Expressing fear enhances sensory acquisition'. *Nature Neuroscience* 11: 843–50.

Young, S.G., Elliot, A.K., Feltman, R., and Ambady, N. (2013). 'Red enhances the processing of facial expressions of anger'. *Emotion* 13(3): 380–84.

Chapter 3

Barsade, S.G. (2002). 'The ripple effect: emotional contagion and its influence on group behaviour'. *Administrative Science Quarterly* 47: 644–75.

Benton, T. (2004). 'Shyness and academe'. *The Chronicle of Higher Education*, 24 May. Available at http://chronicle.com/article/ShynessAcademe/44632/

Cain, S. (2011). 'Shyness: Evolutionary tactic?' *The New York Times*, 25 June.

Chisti, S.-ul-H., Anwar, S., and Khan, S.B. (2011). 'Relationship between shyness and classroom performance at graduation level in Pakistan'. *Interdisciplinary Journal of Contemporary Research in Business* 3(4): 532–8.

Coplan, R.J., et al. (2012). 'Alone is a crowd: Social motivations, social withdrawal, and socioemotional functioning in later childhood'. *Developmental Psychology* 49(5): 861–75.

Daily Mail (2009). 'New iPhone app helps indentify why a baby is crying within ten seconds'. *Daily Mail*, 5 November. Available at http://www.dailymail.co.uk/sciencetech/article-1225555/New-iPhone-app-helps-identify-baby-crying-seconds.html

Derks, D., Bos, A.E., and von Grumbkow, J. (2008). 'Emoticons in computer-mediated communication: social motives and social context'. *Cyberpsychoplogy and Behaviour* 11/1: 99–101.

Eggum, N., et al. (2009) 'Development of shyness: relations with children's fearfulness, sex, and maternal behavior'. *Infancy* 14: 3–325.

Harris, P.L., et al. (September 1987). 'Children's knowledge of the situations that provoke emotion'. *International Journal of Behavioral Development* 10(3): 319–43.

Hughes, K., and Coplan, R.J. (2010). 'Exploring processes linking shyness and academic achievement in childhood'. *School Psychology Quarterly* 25(4): 213–22.

Jayson, S. 'Entertaining emotions: TV may be teaching us to overreact'. *USA TODAY*, 29 June.

Newton, P. (2010). 'From mouse to man: what the latest basic science research is telling us about the human mind'. *Psychology Today*, 3 January.

Paulhus, D.L., and Morgan, K.L. (1997). 'Perceptions of intelligence in leaderless groups: the dynamic effects of shyness and acquaintance'. *Journal of Personality and Social Psychology* 72(3): 581–91.

Planalp, S. (1999). *Communicating Emotion*. Cambridge: Cambridge University Press.

Wolf, A. (2000). 'Emotional expression online: gender differences in emoticon use'. *Cyberpsychoplogy and Behaviour* 3(5): 827–33.

Chapter 4

BBC (2002). BBC news report, Thursday, 24 October 2002.

Crozier, R. (2010). 'The puzzle of blushing'. *The Psychologist* 23/5 (May).

Daily Record (2011). *Daily Record*, 22 April.

Green Flag (2007). 'Road rage affects eight in ten drivers'. //www.greenflag.com/news/press/Road-rage-affects-eight-in-ten-drivers-2007-2-2.html

Landsman, J. (1996). 'Social control of "negative" emotions'. In R. Harré and W. Gerrod Parrott (eds), *The Emotions: Social, Cultural and Biological Dimensions*. London: Sage Publications.

Mann, S. (2013a). *Manage Your Anger*. London: Hodder & Stoughton.

Mann, S. (2013b). 'Does boredom bring out our creative flair?' *Huffington Post* http://www.huffingtonpost.co.uk/sandi-mann/does-boredom-bring-out-out-creative-flair_b_2447393.html
Mann, S. (2013). *The Reader's Digest*, June.
Mann, S., and Cadman, R. (forthcoming). 'Does being bored make us more creative?' *Creativity Research Journal.*
Mental Health Foundation (2008). *Boiling Point: Problem anger and what we can do about it.* London: Mental Health Foundation. Available online at http://www.angermanage.co.uk/pdfs/boilingpoint.pdf
Monk, A., Fellas, E., and Ley, E. (2004). 'Hearing only one side of normal and mobile phone conversations'. *Behaviour & Information Technology* 23/5: 301–5.
Muise, A., Christofides, E., and Desmarais, S. (2009). 'More Information than you ever wanted: does Facebook bring out the green-eyed monster of jealousy?' *Cyberpsychology and Behavior* 12(4).
Sunday Times Magazine (2006). *Sunday Times Magazine*, 16 July 2006.
Tealeaf (2011). 'Tealeaf announces new mobile transaction research conducted by Harris Interactive, shows low consumer tolerance for issues, significant business impact'.
http://www.marketwired.com/press-release/tealeaf-announces-new-mobile-transaction-research-conducted-harris-interactive-shows-1419058.htm.

Chapter 5

Daily Mail (2008). 'Chilling indifference of Italians sunbathing just yards from the covered bodies of two drowned Roma children'. *Daily Mail*, 20 July. http://www.dailymail.co.uk/news/article-1036760/Pictured-Chilling-indifference-Italians-sunbathing-just-yards-covered-bodies-drowned-Roma-children.html
Mann, S. (2002). *Hiding What We Feel, Faking What We Don't.* London: Vega.
Mayer, J.D., Salovey, P., and Caruso, D.R. (2000). 'Models of emotional intelligence'. In R.J. Sternberg (ed.), *Handbook of Intelligence*, pp. 396–420. Cambridge: Cambridge University Press.
Safdar, S., et al. (2009). 'Variations of emotional display rules within and across cultures: a comparison between Canada, USA, and Japan'. *Canadian Journal of Behavioural Science* 41(1): 1–10.
Skinner, B.F. (1953). *Science and Human Behavior.* New York: Macmillan.

Chapter 6

Cahill, L., and McGaugh, J.L. (1996). *Current Opinion in Neurobiology* 6(2): 237–42.

Gabrielsson, A., and Lindström, E. (2001). 'The influence of musical structure on emotional expression'. In P. Juslin and J.A. Sloboda (eds), *Music and Emotion* (Oxford: Oxford University Press), pp. 223–48.

Juslin, P.N., et al. (2008). 'An experience sampling study of emotional reactions to music'. *Emotion* 8(5): 668–83.

Juslin, P.N., et al. (2010). 'How does music evoke emotions? Exploring the underlying mechanisms'. In P.N. Juslin and J. Sloboda (eds), *Handbook of Music and Emotion: Theory, Research, and Applications*. Oxford: Oxford University Press, pp. 605–42.

Levine, L.J., and Bluck, S. (2004). 'Painting with broad strokes: happiness and the malleability of event memory'. *Cognition and Emotion* 18(4): 559–74.

Luomala, H., Sirieix, L., and Tahir, R. (2009). 'Exploring emotional-eating patterns in different cultures: toward a conceptual framework model'. *Journal of International Consumer Marketing* 21: 231–45.

Nauert, R. (2009). 'Emotions Influence Perception of Pain'. *Psych Central.* http://psychcentral.com/news/2009/11/11/emotions-influence-perception-of-pain/9482.html

Schiffman, R. (2012). 'Why people who pray are healthier than those who don't'. *Huffington Post*, 18 January.

Sharp, S. (2010). 'How does prayer help manage emotions?' *Social Psychology Quarterly* 73(4): 417–37.

Van Oudenhove, L., et al. (2011). 'Fatty acid-induced gut–brain signaling attenuates neural and behavioral effects of sad emotion in humans'. *Journal of Clinical Investigation* 121(8): 3094–8.

Chapter 7

Carter, C.S. (1992). 'Oxytocin and sexual behavior'. *Neuroscience & Biobehavioral Reviews* 16:131–44.

Chaplin, T.M., Cole, P.M., and Zahn-Waxler, C. (2005). 'Parental socialization of emotion expression: gender differences and relations to child adjustment'. *Emotion* 5(1): 80–88.

Dittman, M. (2003). 'Anger across the gender divide: researchers strive to understand how men and women experience and express anger'. *Monitor on Psychology* 34(3): 52.

Force, N. (2011). *Humor's Hidden Power: Weapon, Shield and Psychological Salve*. Braeden Press.

Hales, D. (2005). 'The truth about men, their emotions, and ways men can become more emotionally expressive'. *The Reader's Digest*, October 2005.

Kilpatrick, L., et al. (2006). 'Sex-related differences in amygdala functional connectivity during resting conditions'. *Neuroimage* 30: 452-461.

Randall, A.K., et al. (2013). 'Cooperating with your romantic partner'. *Journal of Social and Personal Relationship* 30(8): 1–24.

Schiffer, B., et al. (2013) 'Why don't men understand women? Altered neural networks for reading the language of male and female eyes'. *PLoS ONE* 8(4): e60278. doi:10.1371/journal.pone.0060278

Sladek Nowlis, R. (2000). 'Comparison of anger expression in men and women reveals surprising differences'. http://www.ucsf.edu/news/2000/01/5027/comparison-anger-expression-men-and-women-reveals-surprising-differen

Thomas, S.P. (2003). 'Anger: the mismanaged emotion'. *Disclosures Dermatology Nursing* 15(4).

World Science (2006). http://www.world-science.net/othernews/060403_newsgenderfrm.htm

Chapter 8

Bachorowshi, J.-A., and Owren, M.J. 'Laughing matters', *Psychological Science Agenda*, September 2004.

Blaine, Greteman and Odewire (2009), 'How laughter evolved and how it makes us human'. *Ode* magazine, August.

Diener, E., Lucas, R.E., and Scollon, C. N. (2006). 'Beyond the hedonic treadmill: revisions to the adaptation theory of well-being. *American Psychologist* 61: 305–14. Gilbert, D. (2007). *Stumbling onto Happiness*. New York: Vintage Books.

Harter, P. (2013), 'Can we make ourselves happier?' http://www.bbc.co.uk/news/magazine-23097143

Huffington Post (2013). http://www.huffingtonpost.com/2013/08/23/volunteering-happiness-depression-live-longer_n_3804274.html

Kahneman, D., et al. 'A survey method for characterizing daily life experience: the Day Reconstruction Method (DRM)'. *Science* 306: 1776–80.

Layous, K., et al. (2011). 'Delivering happiness: translating positive psychology intervention research for treating major and minor depressive disorders', *The Journal of Alternative and Complementary Medicine* 17(8): 675.

Lerche Davis, J. (2005). 'The Science of Good Deeds'. http://www.webmd.com/balance/features/science-good-deeds?page=3

Lilienfeld, S., et al. (2010). *50 Great Myths of Popular Psychology: Shattering Widespread Misconceptions about Human Behavior*. Malden, MA: Wiley-Blackwell.

McGhee, P.E. *Humor: The Lighter Path to Resilience and Health.* Bloomington, IN: AuthorHouse.

Moran, C.C., and Massam, M. (1997). 'An evaluation of humour in emergency work'. *The Australasian Journal of Disaster and Trauma Studies* 3: 26–38.

PBS.org (2013). http://www.pbs.org/newshour/rundown/what-makes-us-happy/

Rowe, D. (1996). 'The escape from depression: the secrets of happiness, Part 3'. *The Independent*, 31 March. http://www.independent.co.uk/arts-entertainment/the-escape-from-depression-the-secrets-of-happiness-part-3-1344908.html

Snoep, L. (2008). 'Religiousness and happiness in three nations'. *Journal of Happiness Studies* 9, 207–11.

Vergeer, G., and MacRae, A. (1993). 'Therapeutic use of humor in occupational therapy'. *American Journal of Occupational Therapy* 47(8): 678–83.

Watts, G. (2012). 'Why do some people never get depressed?' http://www.bbc.co.uk/news/magazine-16749565 Watts 2012

Index

Acknowledegements

Chapter 1 Rudolf Höss: Keystone/Getty Images; *Chapter 2* Pan Am flight attendant: Rex Features/Associated Newspapers *Chapter 5* Funeral scene: Russell Underwood/CORBIS *Chapter 6* Man listening to music: Luna Vandoorne/Shutterstock.com